The Illustrated History

Science Fiction
COMICS

•THE TAYLOR•

HISTORY

NUMBER 3

OF COMICS

The Illustrated History

Science Fiction COMICS

MIKE BENTON

TAYLOR PUBLISHING COMPANY
DALLAS, TEXAS

Published by Taylor Publishing Company
1550 West Mockingbird Lane
Dallas, Texas 75235

Designed by David Timmons

**Library of Congress
Cataloging-in-Publication Data**

Benton, Mike
    Science fiction comics : the illustrated history /
Mike Benton.
        p.   cm. — (The Taylor history of comics)
    Includes index.
    ISBN 0-87833-789-X : $24.95
    1. Science fiction comic books, strips, etc. —
History and criticism. I Title. II. Series.
PN6714.B44   1992   91-46777
                                        CIP

Printed in the United States of America
10   9   8   7   6   5   4   3   2   1

Interior photography by
Austin Prints For Publication
Jeff Rowe, photographer

The author gratefully acknowledges the help of the following people who have aided in the development of this book: Laura Benton, Scott Deschaine, Max Lakin, Holly McGuire, Lou Mougin, and Carol Trammel.

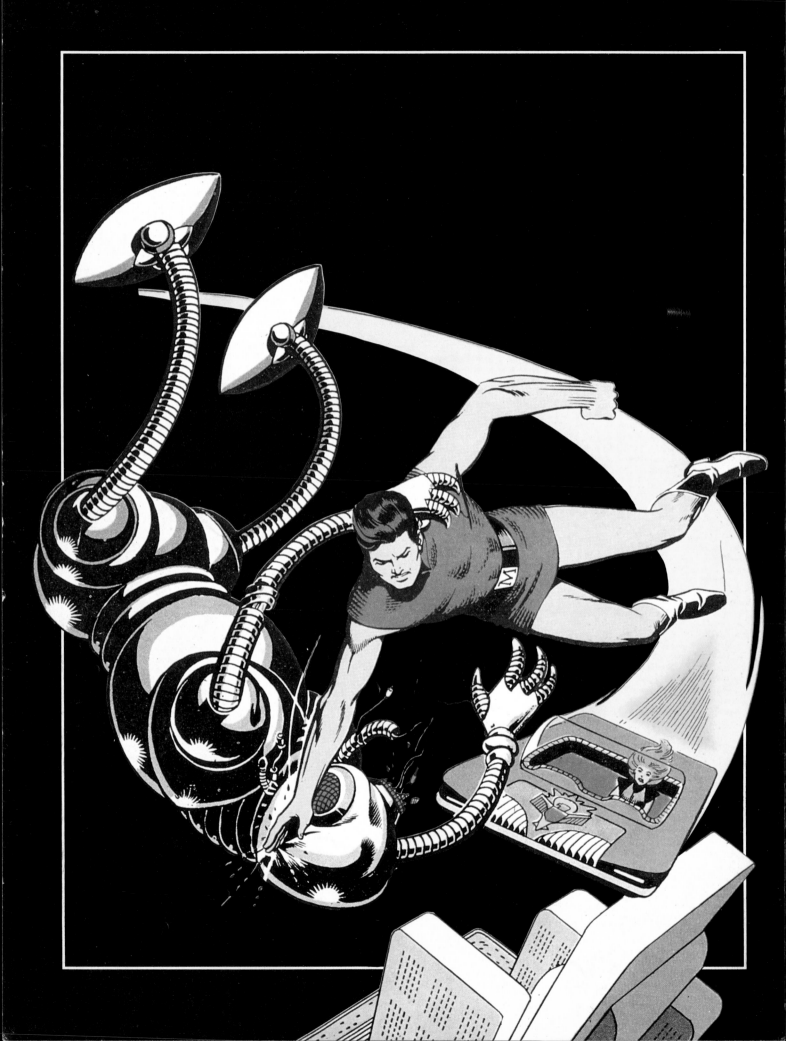

CONTENTS

Facing Page: *Magnus, Robot Fighter #5* © 1964 Western Publishing Co., Inc. Art by Russ Manning.

The Illustrated History

MY OTHER BRAIN IS A SPACESHIP

You're entering another space, another time, another dimension. You're entering the realm of the pure imagination, a place where all possibilities—past, present, and future—coexist. You've been here before, at least in your dreams, or maybe you're already a seasoned explorer. But now you're here. Welcome to the world of science fiction comics.

Buck Rogers in the 25th Century © 1932 John F. Dille Co. Art by Dick Calkins.

For millions of young minds hungry for the most imaginative entertainment that the 20th century could offer, comic books and science fiction were our peanut butter and jelly. In particular, the science fiction comic book became a preferred staple for future scientists, inventors, writers, and artists bent on firing up their imaginations.

Science fiction comics offered many of us the first glimpse of an alternative reality, of a world that finally offered fresh stimulation for our yearning and boundless imaginations. Ray Bradbury experienced that transformation of consciousness which, subtle or not, always seems to occur with the first encounter with science fiction comics. "When Buck Rogers came along," Bradbury recalled, "it was the most amazing thing I'd ever seen—I went absolutely crazy. I lived hysterically waiting for that hour when Buck Rogers came into the house."

Comic books and science fiction have always fed upon each other and have frequently reached the same audiences, with their emphasis on stories of high imagination. In many respects, the science fiction comic book is the most natural expression of the literature of the fantastic and fanciful.

Science fiction, depending upon your definition, may have begun in the Babylonian *Epic of Gilgamesh* (circa 2100 B.C.), or with Mary Shelley's *Frankenstein* (1818), Jules Verne's *Five Weeks in a Balloon* (1863), or H. G. Wells's *The Time Machine* (1895). Science fiction appeared in early 20th-century American pulp magazines like *Argosy* and *All-Story* under the guise of "lost-world romances" and adventure-fantasy stories such as Edgar Rice Burroughs's first magazine serial, "Under the Moons of Mars" (1912).

It was not until 1926, when Hugo Gernsback published *Amazing Stories,* the first English-language science fiction magazine, that science fiction emerged as a distinct and popular genre on the newsstands. Two years later, a story was published in *Amazing Stories* which provided the inspiration for *Buck Rogers,* the world's first science fiction comic strip (1929).

Buck Rogers democratized and spread science fiction to every newspaper-reading home and family. He became the name, by-

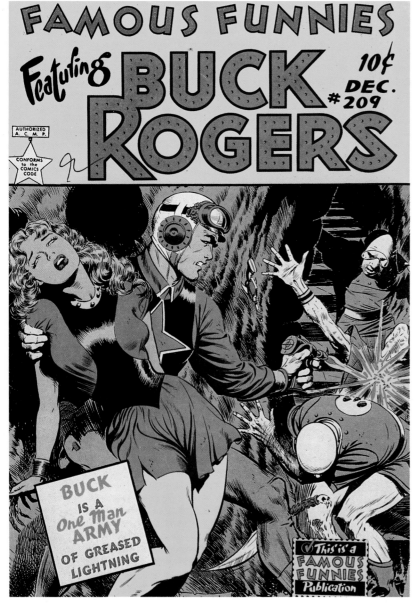

Famous Funnies #209
© *1953 John S. Dille Co.*
Art by Frank Frazetta.

word, and adjective for anything far-out, fantastic, and futuristic—"You know, that Buck Rogers stuff."

Hot upon Buck's space-jets came *Flash Gordon* (1934), a beautifully realized Sunday comic strip series of heroic adventures on the Planet Mongo. Flash completed Buck's work and thoroughly showed us what science fiction could *look* like in the 1930s, whether in Alex Raymond's comic strip or in one of the phenomenally successful *Flash Gordon* movie serials.

The huge popularity of Flash Gordon and Buck Rogers came at the same time that the American comic book was coming into its own, and soon, spacemen with new names were rocketing about in dozens of comic books in the late 1930s.

It can be argued that science fiction was ultimately responsible for the future and success of the entire comic book industry. In 1938, two science fiction fans finally had a character published in *Action Comics* that they had originally created for one of their self-published science fiction fan magazines. Jerry Siegel and Joe Shuster's Superman, an alien from another planet who gains superpowers on Earth, transformed the young comic book industry and launched a lineage of superheroes that stretched through the 1940s, 1960s, and today.

Writers, artists, editors, and publishers all through the 1930s to the 1950s traveled back and forth between working in the science fiction field and in the comic book business. Edmond Hamilton, Alfred Bester, Theodore Sturgeon, Manly Wade Wellman, Henry Kuttner, Leigh Brackett, L. Ron Hubbard, Ray Bradbury, Harlan Ellison, Virgil Finlay, Edd Cartier, Alex Schomburg, and Frank R. Paul all lent their talents in varying degrees to the creation of comic book stories—science fiction and otherwise.

The science fiction comics, with their spin-offs of *Buck Rogers* and *Flash Gordon* movie serials and radio shows, paved the way for science fiction to come to the 1950s television and movie screens. All through the 1930s and 1940s, it had been the comics that defined the visual language of science fiction. Indeed, television shows like *Tom Corbett, Space Cadet,* and movies like *Destination Moon,* were possible because the general public was already exposed to the visual side of science fiction via comic strips and comic books. The science fiction TV shows and movies were so popular in their own right that they were soon adapted for the comic books.

By the 1960s and 1970s, television and movies had become the dominant science fiction entertainment media. The wizardry of special effects in science fiction movies like *2001: A Space Odyssey* and *Star Wars* had eclipsed the visual drama of the comic books. In the 1990s, more people have watched a single TV episode of *Star Trek: The Next Generation* than have read science fiction comic books.

Yet the influence of the science fiction comic book still echoes. It was the comic book which refined, defined, and popularized the standard science fiction themes which repeatedly turn up in movies, television, and books. Flying saucers, little men from Mars, lasers and phasers, space warp and time travel—all the clichés and conventions—have been played out over and over again in the pages of the comic books of the 20th century.

Comic books have long been the indiscriminating repository for all the elements of American pop culture. Movies, radio serials, television shows, and genre novels all filter down (and occasionally up) from comic books. The science fiction in comic books is, consequently, of the most elemental and primary sort. Characters are often caricatures, plots rely on formula, and stories are action driven, with little room for reflection or observation. And therein lies the charm, the appeal, and the strength of the science fiction comic book.

Straightforward and simpleminded, a science fiction comic book story taps into the primal dream state with its exaggerations,

archetypes, and colorful images of "worlds other than our own." Reading a science fiction comic is like being privy to a shamanistic prophesy. You divine the "future" (and, hence, the present) from filtered cartoon images played out in a timeless story of heroics and survival.

With its frozen pictures and simplified drawings, the science fiction comic book creates a two-dimensional view of tomorrow that allows the reader to fill in the gaps—to imagine what goes on between those static panels and breathless lines of dialogue.

Poised between the written word of books and the fleeting visual images of movies and TV, the comic book occupies a pivotal position in the development and popularization of science fiction.

Beyond their role in the development of science fiction as a popular genre, comic books have touched the lives of almost everyone living in the last half of the 20th century. As Isaac Asimov observed, science fiction comics played an important part in preparing society for technological changes because "they presented a dilute science fiction to all levels of the population. The concept of scientific advance became a dim part of the general consciousness, therefore, so that when the time came, for instance, to reach the Moon, enough romance had been created around that theme to make the concept acceptable to the general population."

There you have it: the world today, fashioned by dreamers raised on a diet of science fiction comics. And so let's return to the past—before the days of atomic energy, jet planes, and microwaves—to see how the future came to pass every month, in color, in the world of the science fiction comic book.

Space Adventures #26 © 1958 Charlton Comics. Art by Rocke Mastroserio.

Rocket Ship X #1 © 1951 Fox Features Syndicate.

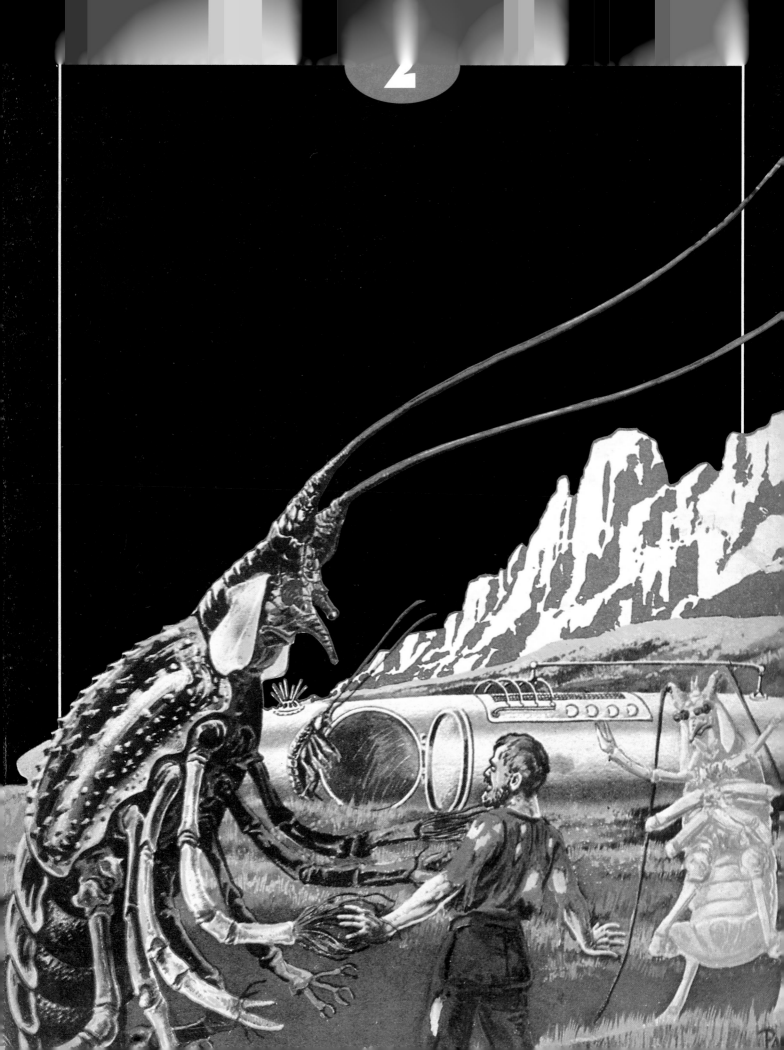

ADVENTURES IN THE 25TH CENTURY

In the 1920s, women cut their hair, hiked their skirts, and smoked in public. Automobiles dueled with horse-drawn wagons and electricity lit farms. Distant neighbors talked on telephones, radios blared a new music called "jazz," and movies began to talk.

Buck Rogers in the 25th Century © 1932 John F. Dille Co. Art by Dick Calkins.

In 1924, astronomer Carl Hubble announced the existence of galaxies outside our own. In 1926, Robert Goddard launched the first liquid-fueled rocket. Stainless steel, electric toasters, and radar were the new marvels.

For the first time, we were living in the future. Gadgets, inventions, technology seized the imagination of people all over the world. There were the dreamers, the schemers, and the popular visionaries, inventors, and mad men. And then there was Hugo Gernsback.

In 1904, at the age of twenty, Hugo Gernsback invented a new kind of battery and emigrated from Luxembourg to the United States in hope of patenting it. A year later, he was publishing a radio catalog and selling home radio kits by mail—fifteen years before the first commercial radio broadcast.

In 1908, he published the first magazine about electricity and radio—*Modern Electrics*. In a 1911 issue, between articles on "Wireless Telegraphy" and a "Photographic Phonograph," Gernsback began serializing a novel he had written called *Ralph 124C 41+*. Set in the year 2660, Gernsback's story was a tour of the technological wonderland awaiting us: vending machines, aluminum foil, and night baseball. His novel also gave an uncanny description of a radar system, complete with diagrams, ten years before it was invented.

During the next fifteen years, Gernsback published stories about the frontiers of science and technology ("scientific fiction") in magazines like *Electrical Experimenter*, *Science and Invention*, and *Radio News*. He even tried to get his readers to subscribe to a proposed magazine in 1924 called *Scientifiction*, but without immediate success.

Gernsback filed away the idea for his "scientific fiction" magazine for two years. In early spring of 1926, he published the first issue of the world's first science fiction magazine—*Amazing Stories* (April 1926). The magazine boasted "Extravagant Fiction Today . . . Cold Fact Tomorrow."

The first three issues reprinted speculative stories of the future by Jules Verne, H. G. Wells, Edgar Allan Poe, and others. The magazine marked the emergence of science fiction as a distinct literary genre, although the actual term "science fiction" would not be popularized by Gernsback for another three years.

Gernsback's readers loved the stories about the marvelous technologies and super-scientific accomplishments of the world of the future, even if the stories were mostly reprints of old favorites. They soon wanted original

Facing page: *Amazing Stories, Vol. 1 #7 © 1926 E.P. Co.* Art by Frank R. Paul.

Buck Rogers in the 25th Century © 1932 John F. Dille Co. Art by Dick Calkins.

stories, however, and Gernsback issued an appeal in *Amazing Stories* for new writers—writers whom "posterity will point to as having blazed a new trail, not only in literature and fiction, but in progress as well."

Writers responded, and the August 1928 issue of *Amazing Stories* featured the first installment of the *Skylark of Space* serial by E. E. Smith, Ph.D., as well as a story called *Armageddon 2419* by Philip Nowlan, a financial writer for the *Philadelphia Retail Ledger*.

Nowlan's story about Anthony Rogers, a 20th-century pilot who wakes up in a 25th

WILMA AND BUCK

Buck Rogers in the 25th Century © 1932 John F. Dille Co. Art by Dick Calkins. Buck Rogers and Wilma Deering ("a pal, not a sweetheart").

"Tonight there comes to us the first of a series of BUCK ROGERS HOURS—of breathless, dramatic adventures IN THE FUTURE—FIVE HUNDRED YEARS from now—when Science shall have bridged the voids of space between EARTH and her SISTER PLANETS—And EARTHMEN, no longer tied to the surface of their relatively tiny world by the bonds of gravity, shall seek their destiny in the CONQUEST OF AN ENTIRE UNIVERSE!"
—Buck Rogers *Radio Broadcast (November 7, 1932)*

century devastated by war, was filled with gadgets, action, and a little romance. Gernsback deemed *Armageddon 2419* a perfect story for his readership and instructed artist Frank R. Paul to illustrate it.

Among the readers who were captivated by Nowlan's story and Paul's illustrations was Chicago businessman John F. Dille, head of the National Newspaper Service. Dille was looking for a new feature to syndicate to newspapers. For a number of years, he had been mulling over the notion of a futuristic comic strip.

"My idea took shape over a period of years," Dille recalled, "and I finally knew that I wanted to produce a strip which would present imaginary adventures several centuries in the future. I wanted a strip in which the test tubes and laboratories of the scientists could be garnished up with a bit of imagination and treated as realities."

Nowlan's story in *Amazing Stories*, as visualized by Paul, provided the catalyst for Dille's new feature. He contacted Nowlan to see if he would adapt his story into a newspaper comic strip, but with only one provision: the hero's name had to be changed from Anthony to Buck. Buck was a good movie cowboy name and movie cowboys were very big in 1928. Nowlan agreed, although somewhat uncertain whether his fantastic story would be suitable for a daily comic strip.

While Nowlan was writing the script, Dick Calkins, a staff cartoonist at Dille's syndicate who originated an aviation comic strip called *Sky Roads*, was now trying to get his boss interested in either a comic strip about the prehistoric past or the old West. Calkins, a World War I Army Air Corps lieutenant, had cut his cartooning teeth at the Detroit *Free Press* before the war and later at the Chicago *Examiner* as a sports cartoonist. Dille took a look at Calkins's dinosaurs and cowboys and decided that the artist's future lay not in the past, but in the future—the 25th century, to be exact.

He assigned Calkins the art chores for the new comic strip. Calkins studied Paul's renditions of Anthony Rogers in *Amazing Stories* and, after a few false starts, succeeded in drawing the world's first science fiction comic strip.

Buck Rogers in the Year 2429 AD appeared in the newspapers on January 7, 1929—nestled between *Mutt and Jeff* and *Little Orphan Annie*. It began as a story of a modern-day Rip Van Winkle:

> I was twenty years old when they stopped the World War and mustered me out of the air service. I got a job surveying the lower levels of an abandoned mine near Pittsburgh, in which the atmosphere had a peculiar, pungent tang, and the crumbling rock glowed strangely. I was examining it when suddenly the roof behind me caved in!
>
> But I didn't die. The peculiar gas which had defied chemical analysis

Buck Rogers in the 25th Century © 1932 John F. Dille Co. Art by Dick Calkins.

preserved me in suspended animation. Finally another shifting of the strata admitted fresh air and I revived. I staggered out of the mine, eager to reassure my parents and friends, but . . . I had slept for five hundred years!

Buck Rogers, a World War I airplane pilot, awakens to a 25th century in the middle of another war. "Half-breed" Mongol invaders are destroying America. Soldiers fly about with rocket backpacks and shoot at each other with zap-guns and disintegrator rays. One soldier is shot down before Buck's eyes.

"Good night! And a girl soldier, too! Say sister, need help? Th' poor kid's hurt—who can she be?"

Buck Rogers in the 25th Century © 1932 John F. Dille Co. Art by Dick Calkins.

Buck Rogers © 1939 John F. Dille Co. Art by Rick Yager.

She was Wilma Deering and she would need Buck's help time and time again in the 25th century. Buck and Wilma crush the Mongol hordes with "exploding bullets" and "ionizing-rays" while jetting about on "sky cycles" and riding in rocket ships that look like angry fire hydrants.

While Nowlan's story about Anthony Rogers reached 100,000 readers in *Amazing Stories*, the *Buck Rogers* comic strip entertained millions of Americans every day. For nearly everyone, Buck was their first introduction to science fiction. As Ray Bradbury observed, earlier 20th-century cartoonists may have "shown the interplanetary wanderings of such characters as Little Nemo. But all that was fantasy. Buck Rogers, now, was the coming reality, fantasy with a vengeance."

Buck Rogers proved enormously popular with a gadget-loving population. After all, the differential-analyzer computer, television-image pickup tube, and electric shaver had all just been invented.

To keep Buck Rogers as futuristically accurate as possible, John Dille consulted with scientists at Chicago University. They suggested to Dille how the space suits in the comic strip could best be constructed so that the moon would not be infected by the germs carried by Buck and other space explorers. Other Buck Rogers inventions included television-controlled rockets, radar-robots, and dome-top cities.

The daily comic strip spun off a Sunday *Buck Rogers* strip in 1930 (initially drawn by Russ Keaton and then by Rick Yager from

Buck Rogers © 1938 John F. Dille Co. Art by Dick Calkins.

"ENLIST!! Help defend Earth against the hostile Tigermen of Mars! Join Buck Rogers Solar Scouts! Be a Space Pilot, Cosmic Gunner, Astro-Observer, Rocketair, Blast Sniper, Radio Operator, Solar Nurse, Secret Space Agent! Write Buck Rogers Earth Office c/o this paper!"

1932 to 1958). The adventures of *Buck Rogers* eventually appeared in nearly 400 newspapers and reached over 50 million readers.

The comic strip inspired a Buck Rogers radio show in 1932 as well as various novelties and premiums. By 1934, kids across the country wanted one toy more than anything else that year for Christmas—a Buck Rogers Rocket Pistol, originally selling for 50 cents. The toy guns gave the English language a new colorful word—ZAP!

The *New Yorker* magazine also took note of Buck's gadgets and super-science adventures that year in its December 22, 1934, "Talk of the Town" section:

> He spends his time in the daily cartoon strip flying around the brave new universe from planet to planet accompanied by one Wilma Deering, a pal (not a sweetheart). With them is a Dr. Huer who invents all kinds of mechanical and chemical and psychic devices to foil, and if possible destroy, Killer Kane and his pal, Ardala Valmar, who is a wretch. Some of the contraptions are rocket pistols, rocket ships, degravity belts, paralysis rays, lightning guns, space suits (which make it possible to step off into space without getting hurt), and an electro-hypno mentalphone for reading the minds of villains and learning their dastardly plots.

Buck Rogers, a bona fide national sensation and media hero by the early 1930s, had already attracted a few comic strip imitators—most notably *Brick Bradford*, which was launched in August 1933. That strip was written by William Ritt, who was reputed to have given his friend Philip Nowlan the idea for the original *Buck Rogers* story. Clarence Gray drew Brick Bradford's adventures, which were often more fantasy than science fiction. Brick engaged in time travel, visited the middle of the earth, and fought dragons and pirates in the Land of the Lost.

Compared to Buck Rogers, however, Brick was not a serious threat and usually appeared in the smaller newspapers. King Features Syndicate decided in late 1933 that it was time to come up with a strip that would give the 25th-century spaceman a run for his antigravity boots.

Alex Raymond, who was drawing the Sunday pages of a boys' adventure strip called *Tim Tyler's Luck* for King Features, was asked to come up with three new strips that could compete with Hal Foster's *Tarzan*, Chester Gould's *Dick Tracy*, and Calkins and Nowlan's *Buck Rogers*.

Buck Rogers in the 25th Century © 1932 John F. Dille Co. Art by Dick Calkins.

Buck Rogers in the 25th Century © 1932 John F. Dille Co. Art by Dick Calkins. Buck's archenemies: Killer Kane and Ardala.

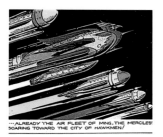

Flash Gordon © 1934 King
Features Syndicate, Inc. Art
by Alex Raymond.

AND THE ROYAL BARGE
OF VULTAN, WITH FLASH,
DALE AND ZARKOV ABOARD,
SETS OUT FOR THE CARNIVAL
OF DEATH!

TO BE CONTINUED

Flash Gordon © 1935 King Features Syndicate, Inc. Art by Alex Raymond.

The twenty-four-year-old Raymond, in a stupendous burst of creativity, brought forth *Jungle Jim*, *Secret Agent X-9*, and *Flash Gordon* in January 1934. Mystery writer Dashiell Hammett wrote *X-9*, but *Jungle Jim* and *Flash Gordon* were conceived and written by Raymond alone. On January 7, 1934, the first Sunday installment of *Flash Gordon* began with a boom:

"World Coming To End!" screamed the headlines. "Strange New Planet Rushing Toward Earth—Only Miracle Can Save Us, Says Science."

In his laboratory, "the scientist Dr. Hans Zarkov works day and night, perfecting a device with which he hopes to save the world—his great brain is weakening under the strain!"

Meanwhile, "aboard an eastbound transcontinental plane we have Flash Gordon, Yale graduate and world-renowned polo player, and Dale Arden, a passenger."

As fate has it, Flash and Dale's plane is struck by a meteor and they must parachute into Dr. Zarkov's backyard. The scientist, his mind snapped from overwork, mistakes Dale and Flash for spies. He forces them at gunpoint to blast off with him in a rocket ship that he has built to deflect the onrushing planet. Flash, Dale, and Dr. Zarkov crash on the Planet Mongo and their continuing adventures then begin in earnest.

Raymond, who borrowed the initial concept for *Flash Gordon* from Philip Wylie's popular book *When Worlds Collide*, constructed a highly stylized view of the planet Mongo and its alien cultures. Never had the world of science fiction seemed so real, so fleshed out, so familiar.

Raymond's *Flash Gordon* took its heroic imagery from the past—Robin Hood, King Arthur, and Beowulf—and borrowed its costumes from the comfortable wardrobes of Lancelot, Napoleon, and Atilla the Hun. And yet, Mongo was also a world of the bizarre and utterly fantastic—populated by Hawkmen, Lionmen, and Sharkmen. Rocket ships fought with horse-mounted warriors, and weaponry could be anything from rayguns to cavalry

Flash Gordon © 1935 King Features Syndicate, Inc. Art by Alex Raymond.

lances tipped with "flaming radium."

In many respects, *Flash Gordon* was more a costume fantasy than a science fiction tale. Gadgets and technology were overshadowed by the romance and color of Mongo. Scenes were more often set in vast medieval halls than in modern laboratories. Flash's archenemy, Ming the Merciless, was the classical Fu Manchu villain of the 1930s instead of an evil super-scientist.

The episodic stories were also pure pulp adventure formula—capture, rescue, and escape. The beginning of the April 15, 1934, Sunday strip gives a summary of a typical adventure:

Flash Gordon © 1935 King Features Syndicate, Inc. Art by Alex Raymond.

Flash Gordon and Dale Arden, two Earth people marooned on the planet Mongo, are separated by the planet's ruler, Ming the Merciless, who wants to marry Dale. Flash makes a friend of Thun, Prince of Lionmen. While Flash is battling the Green Sharkmen in a mysterious city under the sea, Thun rescues Dale. But they are captured by Ming's soldiers. Flash arrives to find Dale gone. Stumbling along the sea bottom, Flash meets Aura, daughter of Ming the Merciless, who leads him out of the sea to safety. The city of the Sharkmen, rising from the sea bed to the top of a mountain, is mysteriously blown to dust before their eyes . . .

Raymond's artwork was more than equal to the task of such grandiose storytelling. Like Hal Foster's *Tarzan*, Raymond's *Flash Gordon* brought a new era of realistic illustration to a Sunday comics page previously dominated by cartoons and caricatures. Anticipating Foster's *Prince Valiant* by three years, Raymond delighted in creating a believable world of heroic figures in a fantastic setting.

"A comic artist," he once observed, "begins with a white sheet of paper and dreams up the whole business—he is playwright, director, editor, and artist at once."

Raymond acknowledged that drawing *Flash Gordon* was demanding: "It takes me four days and four nights to complete a Sunday page. I spend a lot of time while pencilling

Flash Gordon © 1935 *King Features Syndicate, Inc.* Art by Alex Raymond.

Flash Gordon © 1934 *King Features Syndicate, Inc.* Art by Alex Raymond.

in." During occasional power failures, the artist worked by candlelight, never deviating from his self-imposed discipline. In 1935, Don Moore was assigned as scripter to ease Raymond's workload.

By 1936, the popularity of Raymond's *Flash Gordon* prompted Universal Studios to produce a 13-chapter movie serial. Starring Buster Crabbe and filmed on the then-lavish budget of $350,000, the serial became one of the most influential pieces of visual science fiction ever produced.

The success of the 1936 Flash Gordon movie serial prompted two more popular sequels in 1938 (*Flash Gordon's Trip To Mars*) and in 1940 (*Flash Gordon Conquers the Universe*), as well as a Buck Rogers movie serial in 1939 which starred a now back-to-brunette Buster Crabbe.

For the majority of Americans in the 1930s, science fiction *was* Buck Rogers and Flash Gordon. The movies, the newspapers, and the radios carried their daily and weekly adventures to millions of children and adults. From the newspaper comic strips came two characters that would, for good or bad, indelibly define and associate science fiction in the public's mind with the world of the cartoons and comics.

So great an impact did Buck and Flash have on science fiction and on comics, it's tempting to see them as the sole progenitors of all the science fiction comics to come. Besides the two comic strip spacemen, however, the other early major influence in the development of science fiction comics was the science fiction magazines. It was the science fiction magazine artists, after all, who first showed us the future.

Frank R. Paul was the first artist to draw Anthony "Buck" Rogers for Phil Nowlan's original 1928 magazine story in *Amazing Stories*. Beginning with the first issue of *Amazing Stories* in 1926, Paul drew all the covers and most of the magazine's illustrations for the next three years. Paul's early artwork for *Amazing Stories*, and later for *Air Wonder Stories*, *Science Wonder Stories*, and others, exerted an enormous influence over future science fiction artists. Trained as an architect, Paul filled his covers with alien structures, embellishments, gadgets, and cities. Paul's classic vision of the futuropolis, a spired city of tomorrow, became a cliché in hundreds of other artists' reworkings.

In late 1929, a new science fiction magazine modestly called *Astounding Stories of Super-Science* (January 1930) appeared on the newsstands. On its cover, an aviator slugs a gigantic beetle as a bare-legged cave girl shrinks back in terror. Inside was a "complete novelette of adventure in the fourth dimension" as well as the cover story, "The Beetle Horde."

Amazing Stories Vol. 2 #3 © 1927 E.P. Co. Art by Frank R. Paul.

Flash Gordon © 1934 King Features Syndicate, Inc. Art by Alex Raymond.

The artist behind the giant beetle was Hans Waldemar Wessolowski, known as "Wesso" to science fiction readers. He painted all the covers for *Astounding Stories of Super-Science* during its first three years and introduced a sense of action and drama to early science fiction art. Besides giant beetles, Wesso's heroes were also pitted against armor-plated termites, cross-eyed spiders, and a giant amoeba. Adventure, not science, was the main draw for readers of the early *Astounding Stories* and Wesso gave them plenty of alien altercations.

By the time Flash Gordon appeared on the scene, the visual language of science fiction was almost defined. The early science fiction magazine covers provided the first popular images of space cities, space men, space women, spaceships, and space monsters. The increasingly lurid covers of the magazines also attracted a larger, and often younger, audience that was more interested in pure adventure than in hard science.

In 1936, Hugo Gernsback sold his science fiction magazine *Wonder Stories* to Ned Pines at Standard Publications. Pines promptly renamed the magazine *Thrilling Wonder Stories* and tried to make it even more garish and outlandish than *Astounding Stories*. He hired Mort Weisinger, a twenty-one-year-old science fiction fan, to be the magazine's new editor.

For the next five years, Weisinger packaged *Thrilling Wonder Stories* and its compan-

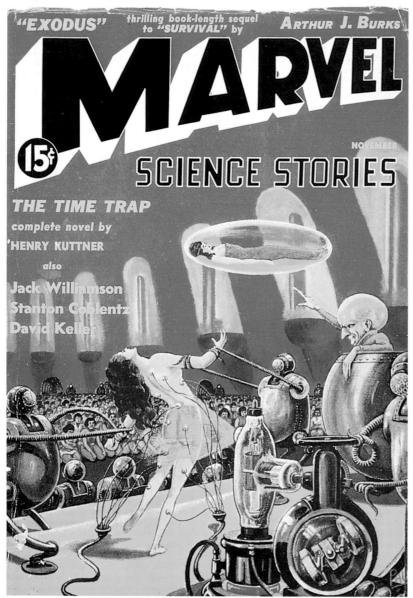

Marvel Science Stories #2 © 1938 Postal Publications. Art by Frank R. Paul.

In 1938, Martin Goodman, a former employee of Hugo Gernsback's and a pulp magazine publisher since 1932, took a shot at the hyperhormonal science fiction reader with *Marvel Science Stories* (August 1938). The magazine featured mildly erotic science fiction stories with slobbering aliens pawing at women in torn lingerie. The first-issue sales of 60,000 copies signaled a vital new market and other publishers took notice.

By 1939, science fiction was enjoying its greatest popularity. The Depression was ending and America was anxious for the future. The New York World's Fair that year took visitors on a tour of the fabulous world of tomorrow ("Futurama—How We Will Live In 1960"). Fans held the first World Science Fiction Convention. And in a supernova display of new talent, a legion of distinguished authors, including Isaac Asimov, Alfred Bester, A. E. van Vogt, Robert Heinlein, Fritz Leiber, and Theodore Sturgeon, all had their first science fiction story published that year.

During the next two years, more science fiction magazines appeared on the newsstands than any time in history. In addition to *Amazing Stories*, *Astounding Stories*, and

ion magazine, *Startling Stories*, to appeal to the growing audience of adolescent readers. The magazine covers by Howard Brown and Earle Bergey emphasized monsters with broccoli-stalk eyeballs, colorful action, and beautiful women. The stories inside were similarly geared for readers somewhere between acne medicine and shaving cream.

Weisinger took a pioneering step and ran a continuing science fiction comic strip called "Zarnak" in the first eight issues of *Thrilling Wonder Stories* (August 1936–October 1937). Drawn by Max Plaisted, the comic strip was a laudable attempt to up the juvenile content of the magazine an extra notch.

Startling Stories Vol. 4 #2 © 1940 Better Publications, Inc. Art by E.K. Bergey.

Flash Gordon © 1934 King Features Syndicate, Inc. Art by Alex Raymond.

Thrilling Wonder Stories, readers could pick up the latest copy of *Fantastic Stories, Startling Stories, Planet Stories, Dynamic Science Fiction, Future Fiction, Fantastic Novels, Fantastic Adventures, Famous Fantastic Mysteries, Strange Stories, Marvel Tales, Unknown, Captain Future, Science Fiction, Science Fiction Quarterly, Astonishing Stories, Comet Stories,* and *Super Science Stories*.

Editors, artists, and writers were quickly pressed into service to fill the demands of the science fiction magazines. Hundreds of stories like "Space-Ship Derby," "Brain Pirates of Mars," and "Planet of the Knob Heads" were wrung out over weekends for readers starved for the blood and thunder of the future.

Buck Rogers and *Flash Gordon* and *Amazing Stories* and *Thrilling Wonder Tales* and all the other early science fiction seemed only to whet our thirst for the future, for the new, the unusual, and the imaginative in our entertainment.

And then one day, on the streets of New York City, appeared the latest marvel and innovation of the 20th century—the American comic book.

ROCKET MEN AND OUTER SPACE QUEENS

In the years of the Great Depression, the Sunday "funny pages" were read out loud by parents to their children who, in turn, would clip and paste their favorite newspaper comic strips into homemade albums. For many Americans in the early 1930s, the weekly comics section was their only full-color entertainment.

Buck Rogers #2 © 1941
John F. Dille Co.
Art by Dick Calkins.

In 1934, Eastern Color Printing capitalized on the public's love of the Sunday comics by reprinting popular comic strips in what became the first newsstand comic book. *Famous Funnies* went on sale in May 1934 and gave readers a second peek at the Sunday comic strip antics of *Joe Palooka*, *The Bungle Family*, *Tailspin Tommy*, and *Hairbreadth Harry*.

With its third issue (October 1934), *Famous Funnies* began reprinting the *Buck Rogers* Sunday strips from the previous year—the first appearance of a science fiction series in the new comic book medium.

The new comic books proved enormously popular, and other publishers issued their own titles of Sunday comics reprints. David McKay Publishing began a line of comic books in 1936 with *King Comics* (April 1936), which reprinted Sunday comics pages from *Popeye*, *Mandrake the Magician*, *Brick Bradford*, *Flash Gordon*, and others.

Comic books soon evolved from a newsstand novelty into the nation's fastest growing periodical item as the 1930s ended. From 1935 to 1940, the number of comic books grew from three to more than 150. There were also now over two dozen comic book publishers and a dwindling supply of available newspaper comic strips for reprinting. The comic books needed new stories and new characters if they were to continue prospering.

Many of the new comic book characters and stories were inspired by successful newspaper strips. When it became time for writers and artists to create original science fiction stories for the comic books, the long shadows of *Buck Rogers* and *Flash Gordon* naturally fell on every page.

The first original science fiction feature in a comic book appeared in 1935, one year after the debut of Alex Raymond's *Flash Gordon*. Instead of "Flash Gordon on the Planet Mongo," comic book readers got "Don Drake on the Planet Saro." Don Drake appeared in the first three issues of *New Fun Comics* (February 1935), the second newsstand comic book ever published and the first with original material.

Facing page: *Planet Comics #54 © 1948 Fiction House.* Art by Joe Doolin.

Clemens Gretter, illustrator of the *Hardy Boys* mystery novels (1932–36), drew the adventures of Don and his girlfriend Betty. Kenneth Fitch wrote this modest epic, which featured Midget Men from Mars and a race of giant ants. The two men also teamed up to produce another science fiction series called "Super Police 2023" for *New Fun Comics,* which featured Rex the future cop and his flying submarine squad car, the "Hi-Lo."

The following year, Greeter and Fitch, now working from the Harry 'A' Chesler shop, created another original science fiction series for the comic books. Their super-scientific "Dan Hastings" first appeared in *Star Comics* (February 1937). The Chesler studio

Flash Gordon #204 © 1948 King Features Syndicate, Inc. Art by Paul Norris.

Rocket Comics #3 © 1940 Hillman Periodicals.

supplied the Dan Hastings series to other comic books over the next ten years. Later adventures were drawn by George Tuska and written by Otto Binder, a science fiction author whose first story appeared in a 1932 issue of *Amazing Stories.*

Binder wrote another early science fiction adventure series called "Mark Swift and His Time Retarder" for *Slam Bang Comics* (March 1939). The time-traveling stories were drawn by brother Jack Binder, who had also illustrated stories written by Otto and brother Earl for magazines like *Astounding Science-Fiction* (November 1937, "Queen of the Skies").

Another early juvenile science fiction comic book series, "Adventures into the Unknown," ran in *All-American Comics* (April 1939) for two years. The stories, adapted from Carl H. Claudy's teenage adventure novels, featured Ted, Alan, and Professor Lutyens in jolly-good yarns like "A Thousand Years a Minute," "The Infra Red Destroyers," and "Rescue on Mars." In their first adventure, the boys take a trip in the professor's antigravity spaceship and fall *upwards* to Mars.

The first costumed space hero for the

comic books appeared in *Amazing Mystery Funnies* (August 1938). Artist Bill Everett took "Buck Rogers in the Year 2429 AD" and came up with "Skyrocket Steele in the Year X." Skyrocket carried a Buck Rogers zap gun—standard weaponry for citizens living in the Year X.

Star Comics (May 1939) tried to give us even more for our dime with stories of "Dash of the 100th Century," certainly four times as good as Buck's mere 25th century. Another early comic book spaceman, "Cotton Carver" (*Adventure Comics*, February 1939), was created for DC Comics by writer Gardner Fox and artist Ogden Whitney and later handled by John Lehti. Also for DC Comics, Tom Hickey wrote and drew the adventures of yet another late 1930s futuristic good guy, "Mark Mason of the Interplanetary Police."

From 1939 to 1941, there were dozens of science fiction series created for the new comic books. The growing comic book medium soon attracted publishers, writers, and artists from the science fiction field.

In 1939, Martin Goodman, who published a line of pulp magazines, including

Startling Comics #49 © 1948 Better Publications, Inc. Art by Alex Schomburg. Alex Schomburg's painted and air-brushed comic book covers were newsstand favorites in the 1940s.

Amazing Mystery Funnies © 1938 Centaur Publications. Art by Bill Everett.

Marvel Science Stories, brought out the first issue of *Marvel Comics* (October 1939). Goodman aimed his new comic book at the same audience that was buying the science fiction magazines and he got veteran science fiction artist Frank R. Paul to draw the cover of the first Marvel comic book.

Ned Pines, another pulp publisher of science fiction magazines like *Thrilling Wonder Stories* and *Startling Stories*, went after the comic book reader in 1940 with a line of comics that included *Thrilling Comics* (February 1940), *Exciting Comics* (April 1940), and *Startling Comics* (June 1940).

The main comic book character in *Star-*

All-American Comics #11 © 1940 DC Comics, Inc. Art by Jon Blummer. Gary Concord stars as Ultra-Man, an early s-f hero, in adventures set in 2239 A.D.

Superworld Comics #3 © 1940 Hugo Gernsback. Art by Frank R. Paul.

tling Comics was named Captain Future, after the science fiction pulp magazine hero created by Edmond Hamilton and Mort Weisinger. Kin Platt drew the Captain's adventures for *Startling Comics* (June 1940). Max Plaisted, the artist of the science fiction strip "Zarnak" in Weisinger's *Thrilling Wonder Stories* (August 1936), also drew for the early issues of *Startling Comics*. Plaisted also helped lauch the "Space Rovers" series in *Exciting Comics* (May 1940).

Other artists from the science fiction magazines were pulled into comic books, as pulp publishers added comic titles to their line. When Hugo Gernsback decided to bring his vision of science fiction to the comic book medium, he hired Frank R. Paul to draw all

three issues of *Superworld Comics* (April 1940). Alex Schomburg, a science fiction artist who had drawn a cover for Gernsback's *Science and Invention* in 1925, also lent his talents to the new comic book industry and drew dozens of covers for comic books throughout the 1940s.

The writers for the comic books were also recruited from the science fiction magazines. Edmond Hamilton, Otto Binder, Alfred Bester, Theodore Sturgeon, Manly Wade Wellman, and Henry Kuttner all wrote comic book scripts. While Sturgeon wrote "comic book continuities to survive," Binder and Hamilton soon discovered that they could earn a better living as comic book writers instead of science fiction writers. Hamilton, whose first science fiction story ("Crashing Suns") was published in a 1928 issue of *Weird Tales*, developed and popularized such standard comic book devices as matter transmitters, flying cities, extraterrestrial robots, accelerated evolution, alien-controlled populations, and the Earth as a living organism. Binder, who had already achieved a reputation for proficiency in the pulps by 1939, would produce more than 50,000 pages of comic book scripts over the next thirty years.

When editor Mort Weisinger left *Thrilling Wonder Stories* and *Startling Stories* in 1941 to work for *Superman* comics, the incestuous mating of science fiction and comics was complete. Editors, writers, and artists were quickly becoming versed and immersed in the language of comic books—the new medium for science fiction.

Although comic books borrowed heavily from the talents in the science fiction field, most of the early comic book science fiction series owed a heavy debt to comic strip artists Alex Raymond and Dick Calkins. From 1939 to 1941, there were dozens of Buck Rogers and Flash Gordon poseurs in the new comic books.

Like Buck and Flash, the comic book spacemen had snappy-sounding names: Power Nelson, Future Man (*Prize Comics,* March 1940); Rocket Riley, Prince of the Planets (*Rocket Comics,* March 1940); and Streak Chandler on Mars (*Top-Notch Comics,* April 1940). Most of the heroes also had a busty and brainy girlfriend and a brawny or brainy sidekick.

Space Smith (*Fantastic Comics,* December 1939) was typical of the early comic book spacemen. He had a "girl companion" named Diana and they were "interplanetary explorers who patrol the far reaches of space to keep shipping and passenger lines clear of marauding pirates." Space and Diana happily shared routine duties like blasting space hijackers and dumping them into vats of melted radium. It was a good working relationship, smart and sensible, as men and women no doubt would be in the future.

Another happy space couple was found in the pages of *Startling Comics* (1947). Lance Lewis, Space Detective, and his professional love interest, Marna, fight such menaces as "Crab Men from Space" and hammer-headed aliens from Mercury. Graham Ingels, who was an editor at publisher Ned Pine's line of Better/Standard comics, wrote the adventures of Lance Lewis, Space Detective:

"Forced to flee Mercury after failing to stop the powerful force beam with which the Mercurians are plunging Venus and Earth towards the Sun, Lance and Marna face the question: Shall they acknowledge failure or persist against hopeless odds?"

Marna: "Well Lance, do we quit or stay on?"

Rocket Kelly #2 © 1945 Fox Features Syndicate.

Startling Comics #45 © 1947 Better Publications, Inc. Art by Graham Ingels. Lance Lewis, Space Detective.

Lance: "For my part, I'd like another crack at that force beam—but I don't want to expose you to any more danger!"

Marna: "If that's your only worry—forget it! We can't let our lives stand in the way of saving the whole Earth civilization! I vote we stay here and try again!"

Thanks to the early role models of the tough and bright women in the *Buck Rogers* and *Flash Gordon* comic strips, the female companions in the early science fiction comic books usually came off better than the "rescue-me" girlfriends in other adventure comic book series.

For example, Ultra-Man (*All-American Comics*, November 1939) of the year 2239 had a girlfriend, Carlotta, who was also Earth's chief scientist—a combination of Dale Arden and Dr. Zarkov. Created by editor Sheldon Mayer and drawn by Jon L. Blummer, Ultra-Man was a futuristic hero in the Buck Rogers tradition in that he was primarily an Earth-based defender instead of a planet-hopping explorer.

On the other hand, most of the early comic book spacemen were interplanetary wanderers—equally at home on the sun-washed beaches of Venus and the frost-packed slopes of Neptune. Whirlwind Carter of the "Interplanetary Secret Service" (*Daring Mystery Comics*, May 1940) bar-hopped his way across the solar system. Similarly, "Rex Dexter of Mars" (*Mystery Men Comics*, August 1939)

All-American Comics #11
© 1940 DC Comics, Inc.
Art by Jon Blummer.

Spacehawk #2 © 1989 Dark Horse Comics, Inc. Art by Basil Wolverton.

did battle from Mercury to Pluto with an array of space-amoebae, plant-monsters, and multiple-cranium aliens.

There were space heroes on Mars, Venus, Jupiter, and the Moon. Heroes of the 23rd century, 36th century, and A.D. 1,000,000. Rocketships full of them. There were so many comic book spacemen by 1940, they were being packed together in crews and legions, like the "Space Legion" in *Crack Comics* (May 1940) and the "Solar Legion" in *Crash Comics* by Jack Kirby and Joe Simon (May 1940). The "Space Rovers" patrolled in *Exciting Comics* (May 1940) while the "Planet Patrol" roved in *Silver Streak Comics* (January 1940). There were even two sets of "Space Rangers" who kept interplanetary law and order in *Mystic Comics* (April 1940) and *Planet Comics* (September 1943).

Although many space heroes were teamed up with companions, there was also the solitary, silent hero who shunned both human and alien companionship. The most rugged individual to emerge from the early comic book space cowboys, space detectives, and space police was the Spacehawk, "a powerful lone wolf champion of law and order thruout interplanetary space" (*Target Comics*, June 1940).

Spacehawk wore a mask in his early adventures and operated as a vigilante ("a super-human enemy of crime who strikes without warning"). His mysterious identity and powers ("I can read your foul thoughts like a book!") struck fear and terror into the hearts of his enemies. Spacehawk was a grim gun-slinger—the dark side of Buck Rogers and Flash Gordon.

In a 1940 story, "Spacehawk and the Vulture Men from the Void," the stern-looking hero captures two Vulture Men. He hogties them together and carries them over to a burning pit. "Now I'm going to rig you two up with just enough anti-gravity power to gently drop you into the crater! If your skins are as tough as your hearts, the gas won't burn you!"

Listening to the aliens "shrieking and writhing in the torments of their own creation," Spacehawk consoles himself with his grim philosophy: "That was an unpleasant job, but that's what I'm here for!"

Basil Wolverton, an outré talent by anyone's standards, was the creator, artist, and writer of Spacehawk. His prior experience as a reporter and cartoonist for the *Portland News* included such assignments as interviewing and sketching murder suspects. One cartooning job which no doubt prepared Wolverton for drawing his space vigilante occurred when an accused murderer "wouldn't pose through the bars for me, so they locked me in the cell with him."

Wolverton, a longtime science fiction fan, broke into comics in 1929 when he sold a newspaper comic strip, *Marco of Mars*, to the Independent Syndicate in New York. Wolverton drew the strip right after the *Buck Rogers* strip first appeared and it seemed destined to be the second science fiction comic. Before *Marco of Mars* was distributed to the newspapers, however, Buck Rogers traveled to Mars in his strip. The manager of the syndicate dropped the strip, according to Wolverton, in order not to appear "we were trying to steal or imitate an idea."

Wolverton's first comic book work came later in 1938 when he drew a short science fiction series for a *Circus the Comic Riot*. His next science fiction series, "Space Patrol," began in 1939 in *Amazing Mystery Funnies* (December 1939–September 1940). Wolverton remembered Space Patrol as "a wild,

Target Comics #7 © 1940 *Novelty Publications.* Art by Basil Wolverton.

weird thing." The extraterrestrial patrol was an alien-lover's delight with Earth "pilot Nick Nelson, his Martian gunner Kodi, and the strange, fierce balloon men of Jupiter."

Wolverton's aliens and alien landscapes made his mind-perverting stories unforgettable. An incredible master of the grotesque (he won a 1946 *Life* magazine contest for drawing the ugliest woman, "Lena the Hyena"), Wolverton peppered his stories with warty, wrinkly people, plants, and rocks.

His aliens often looked like a cross between a gherkin pickle and the male sex organ. His characters clambered in womblike caves and over mammary mountains. Nearly

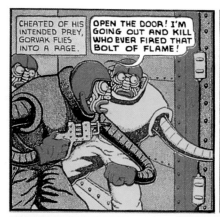

Target Comics #5 © 1940 Novelty Publications. Art by Basil Wolverton.

inative stories. Their imaginations are generally strong, and the stuff fits in."

During the two and a half years Spacehawk ran in *Target Comics*, Wolverton recalled that "it was the feature strip in the book for awhile. Then came the war [1941], and the editor wanted me to bring Spacehawk down to Earth and keep him there."

Spacehawk was snatched from the future and brought to the 20th century. A war was going on and Wolverton's publisher thought it fittingly patriotic that Spacehawk patrol the borders of the USA.

Wolverton recalled, "I had the nerve to argue with him that it would kill the strip. I knew Spacehawk's future was doomed. Anyone with only two brain cells would have known that an interplanetary feature couldn't survive under such a change. It took the zip from the strip to relegate the character to ordinary Earth backgrounds, and so he only lasted a short while thereafter. Within a few months the strip had lost all of its appeal."

Actually, Spacehawk had outlasted many of the other early comic book spacemen. Most of the science fiction series in comic books from 1935 to 1940 were sandwiched every figure, shape, and shadow in a Wolverton story could be broken down into penile or vulval counterparts.

"Sig Freud would probably go raving mad over my stuff," Wolverton said. "I know I draw things that look like all kinds of organs and glands."

Wolverton's deliciously disturbed Spacehawk caused some readers to complain in the comic book's letter column about the monsters being too ugly and the stories "too fantastic."

Wolverton, however, refused to buckle to parents' complaints about his stories. "I was convinced, and still am," Wolverton said, "that young readers lap up powerfully imag-

> "I wrote comics for three or four years [1942–45] with increasing expertise and success. Those were wonderful days for a novice. There was a constant demand for stories, you could write three or four a week and experiment while learning your craft. The scripts were usually an odd combination of science fiction and 'Gangbusters.'" — *Alfred Bester*

Target Comics #6 © 1940 Novelty Publications. Art by Basil Wolverton.

between stories about detectives, cowboys, and early superheroes. This was in keeping with the anthology approach of the early comic books, which tried to offer one type of comic strip for every reading taste. By 1941, however, most of the comic book space heroes were replaced by superhero characters. With the coming of World War II, readers looked for their heroes in the present, not the future.

The other trend was that comic books were now beginning to specialize into genres. Instead of publishing one comic book with a detective strip, a funny animal cartoon, and a wild west cowboy, publishers realized that readers were more likely to buy individual comic books with nothing but stories about detectives, cowboys, or aviators.

One publisher who knew from experience that readers bought strictly by genre was Thurman T. Scott, president of Fiction House. Scott had developed a successful line of genre fiction magazines to please the taste of every 1939 newsstand reader. His magazines, all aimed at specific audiences, included *Fight Stories* (stories about boxers and soldiers), *Wings* (stories about aviators), *Jungle Stories* (stories about a Tarzan clone named Ki-Gor), and *Planet Stories* (stories about adventures on other planets).

Scott's *Planet Stories* (Winter 1939) epitomized the colorful and lurid science fiction pulp magazine. Its covers had the ugliest monsters, the most beautiful women, and the

sleekest spacemen. Stories like "The Beast-Jewel of Mars" and "The Thing of Venus!" promised lots of action, breezy dialogue, and the barest smattering of sense and substance. Perfect material, in other words, for a comic book.

In late 1939, Scott contracted with the S. M. "Jerry" Iger art studio to create a line of comic books based on his pulp magazines: *Jungle Comics*, *Fight Comics*, *Wings Comics*, and *Planet Comics*.

Planet Comics (January 1940) was the first comic book devoted exclusively to science fiction. It was, indeed, the only regularly published science fiction comic book throughout the 1940s. Except for *Buck Rogers*, *Flash*

Planet Comics #57 © 1948 Fiction House. Art by Joe Doolin.

Gordon, and a few other titles, *Planet Comics* established, defined, and dominated the science fiction comic book genre until the end of the decade.

Like *Planet Stories* and its other pulp magazine predecessors and contemporaries, *Planet Comics* relied upon a constant formula for its covers and stories which was succinctly summarized by one reader as "the eternal triangle—the guy, gal, and goon."

Actually, it was the gal who got the most play in *Planet Comics* and in all of the Fiction House comics. Long-legged pinup heroines were in every title and story: Sheena—Queen of the Jungle (*Jumbo Comics*), Tiger Girl (*Fight Comics*), Firehair (*Rangers Comics*), and Cam-

Planet Comics #41 © 1946 Fiction House. Art by Joe Doolin.

Planet Comics #13 © 1941 Fiction House. Art by Zolnerowich.

illa (*Jungle Comics*). For *Planet Comics*, women ran through tomorrow wearing brass bras, latex sarongs, and thigh-high space booties. For adolescent males of all ages, the future never looked more inviting.

Interestingly enough, *Planet Comics* also boasted a sizable female readership who often wrote letters expressing their appreciation for the futuristic femmes. Charlene Stewart of New York wrote in the November 1946 issue that she liked the new heroine Futura because "she has dark hair like my own." Three other female readers wrote a little more incisively about their likes and dislikes, but Jimmy Pittman of San Antonio, Texas, put it to the point: "Put more girls in the stories—hubba hubba stuff."

Not to worry, Jimmy.

One of the earliest and longest-running series in *Planet Comics*, "Gale Allen and the Girl Squadron," was the merest excuse to feature a bevy of beauties. Gale and her girl commando rangers (also known as the "Girl Patrol" and, during the war years, as the "Women's Space Battalion") wore regulation thigh-high space skirts. Gale and her squadron rode the spaceways, looking for pirates and alien slavers, and were often captured,

temporarily, by slimy monsters or heavy-breathing robots.

Another heavy-breathing *Planet* series featured a platinum-haired heroine, Mysta of the Moon. Described in her first story as "a slender girl, alone against the universe's most evil force," she quickly filled out her slender form quite amply. Depending upon the artist who drew her, Mysta wore a different costume from issue to issue but all her wardrobe seemed constructed from vulcanized rubber.

Interestingly enough, one of the artists who worked on the Mysta and Gale Allen stories for *Planet Comics* was Frances (Fran) Hopper—a woman and hence a rarity in the world of 1940s comic book artists. She also drew other Fiction House heroines for *Jungle Comics*, *Rangers Comics*, and *Wing Comics*.

Lilly Renee, another woman artist who worked for Fiction House, drew perhaps the most popular and best-remembered science fiction series in *Planet Comics*—"The Lost World." Renee did not originate "The Lost World" feature; in fact, she took over the strip from Graham Ingels in 1944 and passed it on to George Evans in 1947. She did, however, draw the majority of the stories in this series

Planet Comics #54 © *1948 Fiction House. Art by Matt Baker. Mysta of the Moon.*

Planet Comics #49 © *1947 Fiction House. Art by Joe Doolin.*

about Earth after a successful alien invasion.

In the 33rd century, the warlike men from the planet Volta have destroyed many of the planets in the universe. Earth is left in a shambles and only a few people are left alive to fight the Voltamen.

Two of Earth's last champions are Hunt Bowman, a skilled archer, and Lyssa, Queen of the Lost World. Hunt and Lyssa spend much of their time avoiding and striking back at the Voltamen. The skirmishes between Earth's last survivors and the alien invaders take place among the ruins of the Empire State Building and Central Park—reminders of a conquered and fallen civilization.

PLANET COMICS

*Planet Comics #45
© 1946 Fiction House.
Art by Lilly Renee. The
Lost World.*

"With a force whip we arm her . . . she those who escaped will capture!"

The plots of most of the Lost World stories revolve around Hunt and Lyssa avoiding capture as they inflict horrendous damage upon the Voltamen. One reader complained: "I have been reading the same story in Lost World for the past oopteenth years. I am sure that if I went over the back issues and counted all the Voltamen that Hunt Bowman has killed, I would have enough men for an army the size of Russia's . . . so please have Hunt and Lysa kill them off for all issues to come."

Most of the stories in *Planet Comics* were part of a continuing series. Besides the already mentioned Lost World, Mysta of the Moon, and Gale Allen, other series which appeared and disappeared in *Planet Comics* included Auro Lord of Jupiter (an Earthman's spirit in a Jovian's body), Star Pirate (a space-roving knave with a heart of gold), the Red Comet (a costumed interplanetary hero), and the Space Rangers, starring Flint Baker and Reef Ryan.

One *Planet* series deserving special mention featured the popular heroine, Futura

The pessimistic premise of "The Lost World" was disturbingly attractive to readers who grew up during the uncertain years of World War II with its real holocausts. The Voltamen themselves dressed in uniforms and helmets strikingly reminiscent of World War I German artillery men. The green-skinned aliens also spoke in a broken speech pattern, reversing the objects and verbs in sentences, which made them sound like menacing foreigners or drunken Latin students:

"Blast her, I will!"

"And once her brain numbed is, us she obey will!"

"Look! She an automaton now becomes."

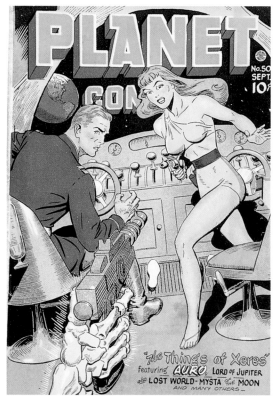

Planet Comics #50 © 1947 Fiction House. Art by Joe Doolin.

Planet Comics #50 © 1947 Fiction House. Art by Murphy Anderson. Star Pirate, the rogue of the space-ways.

written mostly in captions and the stories depended heavily upon the illustration skills of artist Rafael Astarita. Although Astarita's pictures were finely and sensibly rendered, the script often fell all over itself:

Flash of dis-gun and hairy shape crumpling . . . but even Futura's nerve is shaken by the swift attack and close escape. Meanwhile, the shadow-manned search rays are swinging faster in the hunt. Syntho-ghosts as thin as air, but as strong as apes—robots controlled by Men-thor's mind. Now they halt for a frozen instant . . . beyond them a

Planet Comics #41
© 1946 Fiction House.
Art by Joe Doolin.

("Yesterday an Earth-bound secretary—to-morrow a warrior queen!"). The series begins in the 21st century as Marcia Reynolds leaves her secretarial job in Titan City. She has a feeling that she is being stalked by an unseen presence. As her fears increase, she consoles herself with this thought:

"Why should anybody waylay a second-grade technical secretary? No money, no fam-ily—only a norm-plus rating in intelligence quota, energo-efficiency, and mating poten-tial . . . Who'd be after me?"

The answer: A big-brain, green-headed, body-hungry alien from the planet Cymradia named Lord Menthor. Lord Menthor snatch-es the secretary and beams her to his planet where he subjects her nubile body to all types of tests and indignities ("Every cell in my body—probed, measured, and weighed"). The woman is pronounced fit enough for their experiment, Project Survival, and they assign her the lab name Futura.

When Futura learns that the Cymradians intend to use her body as a host for Lord Menthor's brain, she escapes from their clutch-es. Over the next several issues, Futura devel-ops into a strong-spirited fighter as she matches wits against Lord Menthor and his synthetic soldiers. Regal, wild, and always dressed in midriff-revealing two-pieces, Futura served as an attractive role model for girl readers and a pinup fantasy for the boys.

Like *Flash Gordon*, the Futura series was

voice cries out: 'The mud below! It rises up! And look—look!'

The writers of the stories gratefully hid behind house-name bylines. The prolific and nonexistent Thornecliffe Herrick, for example, answered letter columns, wrote two-page text stories, and authored a regular feature, The Lost World.

Jerome Bixby, science fiction author and a writer for the 1960s *Star Trek* television series, wrote for *Planet Comics* from 1948 to 1949 as a break-in to his editorship of *Planet Stories*.

No matter who the writers were—indeed, no matter even which series it was—all the scripts in *Planet Comics* were heavily spiced

Planet Comics #45 © 1946 Fiction House. Art by Joe Doolin.

Planet Comics #50 © 1947 Fiction House. Art by Murphy Anderson.

with a peculiarly 1940s science fiction lingo. To make things sound futuristic, writers smashed words together to create a hyphenated hodgepodge that would have made a military briefing officer proud.

Heroes and villains zapped each other with disintegrating rays fired from "dis-guns" and "dis-cannons." People of the future clocked their time in astro-hours and communicated through video-scopes. There were robo-trucks, nullo-bombs, oxy-machines, hypno-disks, detecto-graphs, mirro-screens, electro-graphs, syntho-slaves, and dyno-lizards.

It was the weapons of destruction, however, that got the most play in the writers' vocabularies. Spacemen wielded guns that shot para-rays, magno-rays, radi-waves, trac-to-rays, blasto-rings, and ato-rays. There was even the sub-sonic, neo-crystal hydra-gun and, for defense purposes, the escapo-hatch.

Like *Planet Stories*, its pulp magazine namesake, *Planet Comics* also had a readers' letters page called "The Vizigraph." The editors explained the purpose of the page by announcing: "Since the art of telepathy is not perfected yet, we request that you resort to the archaic method of communication—letters."

Judging by some of the letters received, it was quickly apparent that not only had the readers not perfected telepathy, they were having a difficult time with any sequential thought patterns:

"I would like to read more stories of our solar system being attacked by races from other galaxies," one jaundiced reader wrote in September 1947, "because one gets so tired of stories that concern our solar system alone."

"What you need," another reader helpfully suggested, "is a girl made of rubber. She'd be able to stand all those ray guns and crazy weapons. The girls in the comic books need more figure, and this girl could have it because she could stretch every which way."

Perhaps rubber girls were stretching things a bit for *Planet Comics*. One reader had already complained about a Star Pirate story because even though "I thought the drawing was swell, I couldn't decide whether to laugh or get upset when the rubber man had Star in his clutches."

It was all in good fun. *Planet Comics* was the epitome of breezy, sexy, mindless, action-filled science fiction. In many respects, the popular 1940s comic book was a throwback to the earlier science fiction magazines and simpler times.

Events, however, were already taking place that would soon push science fiction—and science fiction comic books—into the grim realities of the present.

Rocket Kelly #3 © 1946 Fox Features.

WEIRD SCIENCE, WEIRDER FANTASIES

Science fiction became reality on July 16, 1945, when a man-made nuclear fireball scorched the sands of the New Mexico desert. Three weeks later, the first atomic bomb killed over 80,000 people instantly.

One year earlier, nervous government agents had visited the offices of *Astounding Science Fiction* magazine after editor John Campbell published a story ("Deadline" by Cleve Cartmill) which anticipated the development of the atomic bomb. The agents wanted to make sure that Campbell and his writers weren't somehow privy to scientific secrets of government researchers.

Actually, science fiction writers had nuclear weaponry in their armory even before H. G. Wells's 1914 novel *The World Set Free,* in which civilization was destroyed by atomic bombs. In a 1939 *Buck Rogers* comic strip, six years before Hiroshima, Martians had already dropped atomic bombs on Earth cities.

Still, Campbell was perhaps the most aggressive popularizer of atomic power in science fiction. His first published story in 1930, "When Atoms Failed," explored the possibility of nuclear energy, and was followed by other stories and articles such as "Atomic Power," "Atomic Generator," and "Isotope 235."

When Campbell assumed editorship of *Astounding Science Fiction* in 1937, he began cultivating new writers who could explore themes beyond the monster and spaceman adventures of the other science fiction magazines. Robert Heinlein, one of Campbell's new writers, wrote a 1940 story about a nuclear power plant accident caused by psychological stress ("Blowups Happen") and a 1941 story about radioactive fallout used as a war weapon ("Solution Unsatisfactory").

Heinlein's stories for *Astounding*, along with stories from other Campbell "discoveries" like Isaac Asimov, Theodore Sturgeon, and A. E. van Vogt, explored the human side of science—how technology affected society and the individual. Campbell's *Astounding Science Fiction* magazine soon injected a healthy dose of cerebralism and maturity into a genre that had grown increasingly visceral and juvenile.

To be sure, there were still plenty of zap gun and rocket-ranger adventures in pulp magazines like *Thrilling Wonder Stories* and in comic books like *Planet Comics*, but now there was another type of science fiction—a science fiction that examined the sociological and psychological implications of technological change.

This "after the Bomb," more adult-oriented science fiction would eventually influence future comic book creators who were themselves science fiction readers at the time. In 1946, many of them were out of the service

---

Facing page: Weird Science-Fantasy #24 © 1954 William M. Gaines. Art by Al Feldstein.

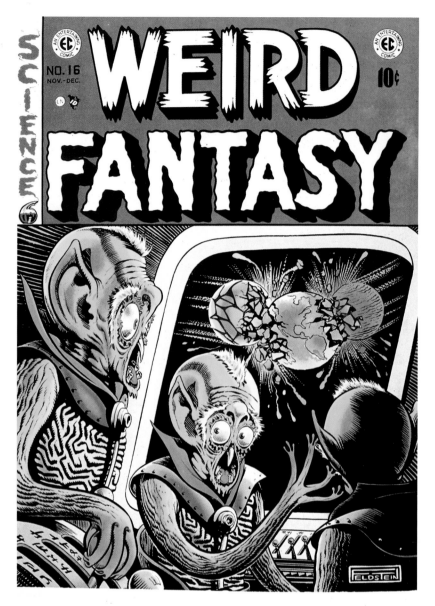

Weird Fantasy #16 ©
1952 William M. Gaines.
Art by Al Feldstein.

1948. "At that time," Harrison recalled, "comics were going great guns—anybody could work whether they could draw well or not. We worked together because neither of us could hack it alone. We were a complete team, we did everything together."

For nearly a year, Harrison and Wally Wood turned out romance stories ("very badly written things") for publisher Victor Fox at $23 per page, payable upon lawsuit. Harrison recalled that "it was too much work for the money. We kept shuffling around, doing a lot of nonsense—one job here, one job there, whoever would buy it."

In a 1949 job-hunting spree, Wood and Harrison walked into the offices of Entertaining Comics (EC). "EC was kind of a small family," Harrison remembered, "only four or five guys there doing all the work." William Gaines, Al Feldstein, and Johnny Craig were some of the guys who did all the work. William Gaines, the publisher, had inherited the comic book business from his father, Max Gaines. Feldstein and Craig were hired as art directors and editors.

Harrison and Wood's romance stories landed them an assignment for EC's *Saddle Romances* (January 1950). When they turned the story in, they were given a couple of stories for EC's western comic, *Gunfighter* (January and March 1950).

While the two men were drawing what Harrison remembered as "chiefly bad western romance stories," Gaines was preparing to overhaul his comic book business. By the end of 1949, Gaines made plans to drop his romance and western titles and replace them with horror comics. While Gaines and Feldstein were plotting their first horror stories, Harrison and Wood were also kicking around an idea of their own.

Harrison was an aspiring science fiction writer and member of the New York Hydra Science Fiction Club. Wood enjoyed doodling spacemen and rocket ships. The two men got an idea. "We just wanted to do a science fiction comic," Harrison recalled, "since there was none of that kind at all at the time."

Harrison recalled that EC publisher William Gaines was "a very friendly guy whose presence encouraged mad things to go on in

and getting an education on the GI Bill. Burne Hogarth, the celebrated artist of the "Tarzan" Sunday newspaper strip, began the Cartoonists and Illustrators School that year for ex-GIs who had aspirations of becoming comic artists. By coincidence, the school attracted a number of young men who were also science fiction fans: Harry Harrison, Al Williamson, Wally Wood, and Roy Krenkel.

Harry Harrison remembered that he and his fellow students were "all living on the GI Bill, seventy-five bucks a month. We mostly bought art books and sold them for cash, keeping just one pencil and a brush." At school, Harrison became friends with Wally Wood and the two began drawing together in the office, footprints on the ceiling, that sort of thing. He was always open to suggestions, so somewhere along the line I gave Gaines a lot of science fiction to read. We [Wally Wood] tried to talk him into starting a science fiction comic."

The two men were successful. One month after launching his new horror comic line, Gaines premiered EC's two new science fiction comics, *Weird Science* (May 1950) and *Weird Fantasy* (May 1950).

Gaines's two new comics grew out of a different science fiction tradition than Flash Gordon and *Planet Comics*, borrowing more from the influence of John Campbell and his stable of writers at *Astounding Science Fiction*. Harrison recalled that "the EC science fiction weren't as pulp-magazine-adventure slanted. They tried a little bit different type of science fiction from the rest of the field."

As far as comics were concerned, *Weird Science* and *Weird Fantasy* began a new era in science fiction. In retrospect, Gaines acknowledged that EC "started what we called real science fiction as opposed to cowboys-and-Indians-in-spaceships science fiction like Buck Rogers."

Weird Science #9 © 1951 *William M. Gaines.* Art by Wally Wood.

THE SCIENTIST WHO IS PRACTICING HIS SPEECH BEFORE HIS WIFE FOLLOWS HER GLANCE OUT OF THE WINDOW AND INTO THE NEW MEXICO NIGHT SKY...

LOOK, GEORGE! THAT LIGHT... IN THE SKY! IT'S MOVING...

BUT ...NOBODY FLIES ANYMORE! IT MUST BE...

THE LIGHT GROWS BRIGHTER! SOON ITS SOURCE IS CLEARLY VISIBLE...

GEORGE! IT'S...IT'S A FLYING SAUCER!

GOOD LORD! IT'S LANDING!

THE WEIRDLY SHAPED CRAFT SLIPS EARTHWARD AND COMES TO REST NEAR THE SCIENTIST'S HOME...

THEY'RE AFTER ME, SARAH! THEY'RE AFTER ME BECAUSE I'M RIGHT!

THE THINGS COME FROM THE DISC-SHAPED SHIP! THEY MOVE SWIFTLY... SILENTLY...

GEORGE! LOCK THE DOORS! QUICKLY! BOLT THE WINDOWS!

IT...IT WOULDN'T DO ANY GOOD, SARAH!

GEORGE IS RIGHT! THE HEAVY FRONT DOOR MELTS AWAY AS THE THINGS COME THROUGH...

THEY'RE GOING TO KILL US, SARAH! KILL US FOR WHAT WE KNOW!

OH, GEORGE, SOB! GEORGE!

DEATH COMES SWIFTLY TO THE SCIENTIST AND HIS WIFE...

AND AS THE SILVERY DISC HURTLES SKYWARD, A THIN WHISP OF SMOKE RISES FROM THE TINY RANCH HOUSE'S CHIMNEY! INSIDE, A FLICKERING FLAME DIES! THE REPORTS ...THE RESEARCH ...THE THEORIES...LIE IN A NEAT PILE OF BLACK ASHES...

THE END

Weird Science #16 © 1952 *William M. Gaines.* Art by Wally Wood. From "Down to Earth."

The stories in *Weird Science* and *Weird Fantasy*, like the EC horror comics, were usually coplotted by Gaines and Feldstein, and then scripted by Feldstein for the artists to draw. Gaines recalled that "Al and I enjoyed writing the science fiction the most. I guess we felt more intellectually stimulated, and we believed we were reaching an older and more intelligent group of readers."

Feldstein remembered that "when we were working on the science fiction, we would spend hours on theory—on just developing the time loop stuff that we did, for example, to make sure it worked exactly right, and that it was perfectly logical that this guy who went up on the Titanic to stop the disaster was the throughout the entire history of EC's science fiction stuff."

Like other science fiction at the time, the EC comics wrestled with the moral and technological implications of the new atomic age. In 1951, the first *hydrogen* bomb exploded at the time Feldstein and Gaines were creating the science fiction comics. Feldstein recalled that "now here was this terrible, terrible weapon . . . if there was going to be war it was going to be complete annihilation suddenly. That was the kind of thing that was in the back of our mind when we referred to the bomb in our science fiction stories. It was because we had great concern about it."

Such concern prompted Feldstein to write and draw "Destruction of Earth" for *Weird Science* #14, which was voted the most popular story of the issue by the readers. This chilling nuclear annihilation tale set the pace for other "ultimate catastrophe" stories that followed: "The Radioactive Child" (*Weird Science* #15), "Spawn of Venus" (*Weird Science* #6), and "Cosmic Ray Bomb Explosion" (*Weird Fantasy* #14).

In another postholocaust story, "Child of

Weird Science #5 © 1951 William M. Gaines. Art by Al Feldstein.

guy who caused it. And if he hadn't been there in the first place, it wouldn't have happened. "

The EC science fiction stories were carefully plotted to deliver a surprise-twist ending with a heavy helping of irony and cynicism. Since they were aiming for an older audience, Gaines and Feldstein used their science fiction stories to make statements about such 1950s issues as nuclear disarmament, racial prejudice, and male-female relationships.

As Gaines observed, "science fiction traditionally has been a great vehicle for an author to try to teach a moral or ethical lesson, and we were certainly doing that

Weird Science #14 © 1950 William M. Gaines. Art by Al Feldstein.

Tomorrow" (*Weird Fantasy* #17, 1951), only one human survivor is left in a world now populated by radioactive mutants. The final bitter irony of the story comes when he must kill one of the vicious mutants, only to discover that it had once been his only child.

Next to nuclear holocaust, however, the biggest concern of EC's adolescent readers was the opposite sex. Like much other science fiction of the day, the EC comics pandered to male adolescent fantasies and daydreams. Boys fresh on the threshold of puberty delighted in stories about future sex, alien sex, and weird sex.

One story that turned up more than once was the "build your own babe" fantasy. For example, in *Weird Science* #5 ("Made of the Future!", January 1951), a man stumbles into the "future" and discovers a store that sells "A Construct-A-Wife Kit."

Our sweaty-palmed protagonist selects the "Delux Kit B-5." The saleswoman, dressed appropriately in a transparent nightgown, tells him that the "B-5" stands for a blonde model, five feet, five inches. She also assures him that "the Delux Kit provides you with a delux wife! Never nags, never argues, doesn't object to your staying out late with the boys . . . always cooks, always smiles . . . cooks divinely, sews, adores you completely . . . obeys your every command! In other words, the perfect wife!"

Hurrying home, he mixes the kit's ingredients in his bathtub. A body, obviously female, begins to grow before his eyes. "I was a little embarrassed as the form took shape! She was *beautiful*! I went into the bedroom and brought a blanket which I placed over her. . . . "

The idea of future technology neatly solving such a messy issue as sex was certainly appealing to readers who might be struggling with their own emerging sexuality. Several months later, the story was repeated again in *Weird Science* #15 (September 1952).

Melvin Sputterly, a homely bachelor, accidentally receives a package from the future. Melvin tears open the wrapping paper and "inside was a gayly colored box with a picture of several scantily clad beautiful women upon it! Melvin gasped! The words above the pictured screamed at him. . . . Delux Personal

Weird Fantasy #15 ©
1952 William M. Gaines.
Art by Jack Kamen.

Harem Kit. Not to be sold to Minors or Married Men. This rule strictly enforced!"

Sputterly reads the instructions: "Guaranteed to contain five of the most beautiful harem girls ever dehydrated! Upon hydration, each girl will fall madly in love with you!"

Like all EC stories, however, this bowl of cherries was full of pits. As Melvin tries to bring each harem girl to life (again in the bathtub), he botches the rehydration process. Sexually thwarted, he ends up in the clutches of his spinster neighbor.

Sexual frustration and betrayal was one of the most common themes in the EC horror comics, with countless cuckold corpses returning from their graves to kill cheating spouses and murderous lovers. In the EC science fiction comics as well, sex was always presented as either unobtainable or fraught with unforeseen perils.

For example, in the story "There'll Be Some Changes Made" (*Weird Science* #14), a groom discovers that his new bride is actually an alien Gastropodian. Being biologically compatible, there doesn't seem to be a problem until he notices that his wife starts growing a beard. Gastropodians, she/he tells him, *change* sex for the second half of their lives. Oh.

Another problem with hormones is ex-

Weird Science #22 © 1953 William M. Gaines. Art by Al Williamson, Frank Frazetta, Roy Krenkel. From "A New Beginning."

Weird Science-Fantasy #27 © 1955 William M. Gaines. Art by Wally Wood.

plored in "Transformation Completed" (*Weird Science* #10). To keep a man from marrying his daughter, an angry father injects him with a powerful dose of *female* sex hormones, which turns him into a her. Just to show Daddy he can't ruin her wedding, the bride-to-be injects herself with *male* hormones and becomes the groom.

If a marriage should go smoothly in an EC comic, even consummation can never be taken for granted. In *Weird Science* #19 ("Right on the Button"), a man and woman on their wedding night begin to undress for bed. Suddenly the wife looks at her husband in horror and grabs a hat pin. She stabs him in the chest repeatedly and without warning. "He screamed as I drove it in. I felt it tear flesh, crunch against cartilage. I raised it and stabbed again and again . . . "

When the police question her, the woman pulls up her dead husband's shirt: "I pointed to the spot below Lon's chest . . . below the torn flesh and blood . . . Look. A *navel*. He had a *navel*."

The policeman gasps: "*Incredible!* He was a *mammal!*"

The woman nods. "Where he came from, the superior race is the *mammal*, which bears its young alive . . . attached to the mother by an umbilical cord . . . and here, we lay *eggs*! We *have no navels*!"

Another persuasive argument against interspecies marriage occurs in *Weird Science* #10 ("The Maidens Cried"). On a distant planet, a crew of Earthmen discovers a race of beautiful women who are all alone. Seduction and mating follows. The Earthlings, however, soon discover why there are no other men on the planet. It seems that the impregnated women must reproduce by laying their fertilized eggs *inside* their human lovers. The men's bodies served as the food hosts for their offspring. Daddy, it seemed, was going to be delicious.

A world full of women without men also appeared in the story " . . . For Posterity" (*Weird Science-Fantasy* #24). The radioactive aftermath of an atomic holocaust causes only women to be born. Soon there are no more males and the race is in danger of dying. A woman doctor, however, discovers a chemical that makes it possible for "the female patient to effect the reproductive method

Weird Science #22 © 1953 William M. Gaines. Art by Wally Wood.

known as parthenogenesis . . . self-fertilization!"

Women fertilizing themselves was a daring topic for a comic book—especially one in the early 1950s. While young minds grappled with such an astounding possibility, the doc-

THE WOMAN STARED AT HERSELF IN THE CONTROL PANEL, LISTENING TO THE NIGHT SOUNDS...TO THE MAN SLEEPING ACROSS THE CLEARING...

THIS IS *WRONG!* THIS IS THE *BASIC EVIL!* A WORLD WITHOUT *LOVE* IS A *WORLD OF EVIL.* THIS METHOD OF *PROPOGATION* IS WRONG...

Weird Science #22 © 1953 William M. Gaines. Art by Al Williamson, Frank Frazetta, Roy Krenkel.

Weird Science-Fantasy #24 © 1954 William M. Gaines. Art by Joe Orlando.

In a story called "He Walks among Us" (*Weird Science* #13, May 1952), William Gaines and Al Feldstein came up with a Christ fable set on another planet. A space explorer in the year 2963 arrives on a planet with a culture and society much like Earth's of 3,000 years ago.

He assumes the clothing and manners of the local people and blends in with them. Later, he uses his advanced knowledge and scientific gadgets to perform such seeming miracles as healing the dead and turning water into milk. The highly religious people of the time look upon the Earthman as their savior.

The jealous priests, however, see this new savior as a threat and have him tortured upon a rack and killed. His death inspires a new religion and his followers wear small wooden "racks" around their necks to show their faith.

Readers made the easy connection to Christianity and most of them didn't like it. The letter column was filled with comments like "offensive, let's not have any more like it . . . that story openly attacks the Christian religion . . . insults the reader."

Gaines and Feldstein, however, were simply breaking new ground. While the story may have been partially inspired by Ray Bradbury's 1949 story about an interplanetary Jesus ("The Man"), it was also EC's own way of provoking the reader to think and to question even the most fundamental beliefs.

Having staked out positions on the 1950s issues of nuclear disarmament, sex, and religion, the EC science fiction comics were also equally willing to make moral statements about bigotry, prejudice, and racial inequality. Alien races were often used in the EC science fiction comics to make a point about our own racism on Earth.

For example in "The Teacher from Mars" (*Weird Science-Fantasy* #24), Earth boys hate their Martian teacher out of blind prejudice ("You're Martian scum . . . we've never had a Martian teacher before and we don't want one now!"). In "The Mutants" (*Weird Fantasy* #10), people of the future enforce a rigorous and unreasonable segregation to keep genetic freaks out of "normal" society.

Even interracial marriage was treated in a

tor in the story lays it out in details that would have made a health teacher proud: "Parthenogenesis will only produce females! The chemical artificially activates the ovum. In the old days, the male sperms contained X or Y sex chromosomes. The female ovum, only Y. If Y united with Y—YY—the results were female! X with Y—XY—Male! Artificial activation doubles the egg's sex chromosomes . . . Y to YY . . . Female!"

Obviously, after discussing the chromosome content of the male sperm, the EC science fiction comics weren't afraid to tackle other taboo topics of the 1950s, and offered controversial looks at religion and Christianity.

daringly sympathetic story ("Close Shave") written by Otto Binder for *Weird Science-Fantasy* (February 1955):

In the future, a race of apelike aliens called Ganymedes emigrate to Earth to find employment. Trouble arises when the aliens try to integrate themselves into our society as equal members. The Ganymedes, some people suspect, may even be secretly marrying into the human race.

A TV announcer tells the public that "the Ganymedes are quite humanlike, biologically. Offspring born of Ganymedes and humans are perfectly normal. However, the hairy fur cover of a Ganymede is a dominant characteristic. If we were to allow Ganymedes to pass into our society, the smooth-skinned human would vanish as a race!" (The word "pass" was sometimes used in the 1940s and 1950s to signify a light-skinned black person who was "passing" for white.)

Another critic also issues a warning about "Ganymedes, with their hairy fur removed, posing as Earth humans. We must stop this secret mingling of Ganymedes into our society. We must preserve the purity of the human race. These Ganymedes are nothing but apes!"

A young woman who hears the TV news thinks to herself: "Bigots! Intolerant idiots! Same old story . . . racial intolerance. They were originally imported as cheap labor, underpaid, miserable, restricted to the poorest housing areas. How else could they ever better themselves than by trying to pass into human society?"

Later in the story, the woman falls in love with a man who shamefully confesses to her that he is a Ganymede who has "passed" by shaving off all his body fur. He is afraid now that she will think he wanted to marry her just to become part of the human race. Instead of rejecting his offer of marriage, the woman accepts. She tells him (untruthfully) that she is also secretly a Ganymede who is "passing" for human, so there is no need for prejudice to come between them.

EC's strongest statement about racial intolerance came in a story called "Judgement Day" (*Weird Fantasy* #18). An Earthman in the far future travels to a planet inhabited entirely by two types of mechanical citizens:

Orange Robots and Blue Robots. He notices that the Orange Robots live in nice houses and go to good schools. Meanwhile, the Blue Robots are segregated in a poor part of town and have to ride in the back of buses.

The Earthman points out these inequities to an Orange Robot and tells him that the coloring of their metal sheathing is the only real difference between him and the Blue Robots. The Orange Robot protests: "This existed before I was born! What can I do about it? I'm only one robot."

The Earthman replies that such conditions once existed on Earth, but after "mankind learned to live together, real progress first began, and the universe was suddenly

Weird Fantasy #14
© 1952 William M. Gaines. Art by Wally Wood.

Weird Science #22 © 1953 William M. Gaines. Art by Wally Wood.

SF EC Bradbury

"The Rocketman" and "Kaleidoscope"
("Home to Stay")
Weird Fantasy #13 (May 1952)
"There Will Come Soft Rains . . . "
Weird Fantasy #17 (January 1953)
"The Long Years!"
Weird Science #17 (January 1953)
"Mars Is Heaven!"
Weird Science #18 (March 1953)
"Zero Hour"
Weird Fantasy #18 (March 1953)
"King of the Grey Spaces!"
Weird Fantasy #19 (May 1953)
"The One Who Waits"
Weird Science #19 (May 1953)
"Changeling" ("Surprise Package")
Weird Science #20 (July 1953)
"I, Rocket"
Weird Fantasy #20 (July 1953)
"The Million Year Picnic"
Weird Fantasy #21 (September 1953)
"Punishment without Crime"
Weird Science #21 (September 1953)
"Outcast of the Stars"
Weird Science #22 (November 1953)
"The Silent Towns"
Weird Fantasy #22 (November 1953)
"The Flying Machine"
Weird Science-Fantasy #23 (March 1954)
"A Sound of Thunder"
Weird Science-Fantasy #25 (September 1954)

(Note: Other Bradbury adaptations appeared in the EC horror and crime titles: *Vault of Horror* #s 22, 29, 31; *Haunt of Fear* #s 16, 18; *Tales from the Crypt* #s 34, 36; *Crime Suspenstories* #s 15, 17; *Shock Suspenstories* #s 7, 9.)

Weird Fantasy #17 © 1952 William M. Gaines. Art by Al Feldstein.

ours." It is only at the end of the story that the visiting Earthman is revealed to be black.

Many writers wrote to praise the story, including Ray Bradbury, who thought the story "should be required reading for every man, woman, and child in the United States." It was still 1953, however, and one reader wrote: "I am not prejudiced, so I was not offended by 'Judgement Day,' but some of my best friends were . . . why not leave well enough alone?"

The EC science fiction comics dared to make their readers think and question some of their most basic beliefs by showing the "other" side of an issue. In a story called "The Probers" (*Weird Science* #8), aliens dissect human beings to see how "lower forms of life functioned"—just as humans do to laboratory animals. In "Bum Steer!" (*Weird Science* #15), men are abducted by a flying saucer and then fattened up for slaughter—just as cattle are by ranchers. In "Revulsion" (*Weird Fantasy* #15), giant grasshoppers scream in horror when they find a human in their salad.

Humanity, in general, was not treated too kindly in the EC science fiction comics. Unlike *Buck Rogers* or *Flash Gordon,* in which technology or personal heroism could conquer the perils of the future, the EC stories frequently showed humans beaten at their own game and done in by their own foibles. Gaines acknowledged that the cynicism in the stories came "probably from a belief on my part that People Are No Damn Good. This was a well known strain that you'd see running through a lot of science fiction stories, that the whole galaxy was so disgusted with Man that they would isolate him."

Besides coming up with about four science fiction stories every month, Gaines and Feldstein were at the same time plotting the horror, suspense, and crime comics. They searched everywhere for ideas that could be turned into comic book stories.

Gaines remembered that "before we got to the point where we could do our own plotting, we were lifting plots that we remembered from things we had read many years before in the pulps, never dreaming that anybody would ever recognize them. I remember the very first story in *Weird Science* #12, which was the first science fiction issue we ever published. It was called 'Lost in the

Weird Fantasy #15 © 1952 William M. Gaines. Art by Al Feldstein.

"I think my writing is intriguing to a lot of people because I make pictures on paper for them, and they're all based on my comic-collecting background and love of illustration."
— Ray Bradbury

Weird Fantasy #20 © 1953 William M. Gaines. Art by Al Feldstein.

Microcosm.' I lifted it from something I read twenty years earlier, when I was like a ten-year-old kid, that I read in *Amazing* or *Astounding Stories.* How the hell did I know that I was lifting a classic that everybody in science fiction knows as 'He Who Shrank'?"

Consciously or not, Feldstein and Gaines also borrowed liberally from other writers. Fritz Leiber's "Nice Girl with Five Husbands" appeared as "A Timely Shock" in *Weird Fantasy* #10; ditto for Ralph Milne Farley's "Liquid Life" (*Weird Fantasy* #11 as "The Jar") and A. E. van Vogt's "Far Centauris" (*Weird Fantasy* #15 as "The Long Trip").

Other writers given the EC treatment included Fredric Brown, Anthony Boucher,

Weird Science #17 © 1953 William M. Gaines. Art by Wally Wood.

was published under the title "Home to Stay" in an issue of *Weird Fantasy*.

A few weeks later, they received the following letter:

> Dear Sir:
>
> Just a note to remind you of an oversight. You have not as yet sent on the check for $50.00 to cover the use of secondary rights on my two stories, "The Rocket Man" and "Kaleidoscope" which appeared in your *Weird Fantasy* May–June '52 No. 13, with the cover-all title of 'Home to Stay.' I feel that this was overlooked in the general confusion of office work and look forward to your payment in the near future. My very best wishes to you,
>
> Ray Bradbury

Gaines promptly sent him a check and an agreement which led to the authorized adaptations of twenty-four more stories.

Bradbury's gentlemanly response and agreement to the use of his work was no doubt influenced by the classy treatment given his

Damon Knight, John Collier, William Hope Hodgson, Roald Dahl, Richard Matheson, Katherine MacLean, Nelson Bond, and Edgar Allan Poe.

And then there was Ray Bradbury.

In 1950, Bradbury was a rising star in the skies of science fiction and fantasy. His short story collection, *The Martian Chronicles*, was published to critical acclaim and was quickly followed by *The Illustrated Man* (1951).

In 1952, Gaines and Feldstein took two Bradbury stories from *The Illustrated Man*, tacked the beginning of one onto the end of the other, and gave their patchwork adaptation to Wally Wood to illustrate. The story

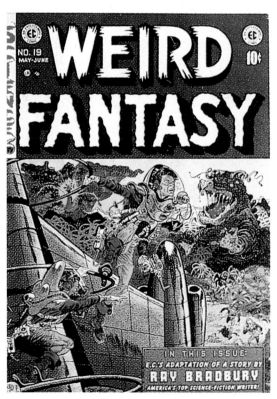

Weird Fantasy #19 © 1953 William M. Gaines. Art by Joe Orlando.

stories by EC. Al Feldstein, who adapted all but one of the Bradbury stories for EC, preserved Bradbury's style, while streamlining it for a visual medium.

"The story was all there," remembered Wally Wood, who illustrated "Home to Stay" and several other Bradbury stories. "There were less words. It got the feeling, and it translated very well into comics."

Bradbury, a longtime comics fan, was also pleased by the skillful treatment given his stories by the EC artists. He wrote a letter to the staff in 1953 to express "nothing but the highest regard and love" for their adaptations so "beautifully and handsomely and cleverly thought out and completed! Long may we all work together!"

At the same time, Bradbury had some concern for his new popularity in the comic books. "My name was appearing on the covers of more and more and yet more covers of EC magazines," Bradbury recalled, "and my first films were beginning to appear. I was given the task of adapting into screenplay form the incredible *Moby Dick*, directed by John Huston. I knew of the rampant snobbism in the world concerning comic strips of any sort. I lived in some faint fear of someone in the film complex where I was working speaking up and saying something like 'Bradbury? Say, isn't he the guy who writes for those cheap comic books?'"

If Bradbury's peers, however, had peeked behind the covers of the "cheap comic books," they would have perhaps seen for themselves what EC comic book readers already knew: *Weird Science* and *Weird Fantasy* were not only some of the best *written* but also the best *illustrated* comic books ever produced.

After his EC comic book stories were collected and published in a series of 1960s paperbacks, Bradbury stated that "I am indebted to the artists who illustrated my work for EC. I am happy to have their work collected in two books now by Ballantine. I no longer have to sneak around in the shadows with them, fearful of the criticism of snobs. We have come out in the light, all of us. And the sun feels good, doesn't it, fellows."

The fellows who joined Bradbury in the sunlight were Wally Wood, Al Williamson, Joe Orlando, Frank Frazetta, Roy Krenkel,

Weird Fantasy #17 © 1952 William M. Gaines. Art by Wally Wood. Ray Bradbury adaptation.

John Severin, Bill Elder, George Evans, Reed Crandall, Jack Kamen, Al Feldstein, and Harvey Kurtzman—the main artists who worked on the EC science fiction titles.

Wally Wood, who had helped convince Gaines to launch *Weird Science* and *Weird Fantasy*, soon became the preeminent 1950s science fiction comic book artist. He drew complex spaceships, alien landscapes, outerspace monsters, and perfectly poised women in the same glossy and tightly polished style. He knew how to make the sun glint off a space helmet.

Wood drew over fifty EC science fiction stories, in addition to his work on the other EC comics, including *Mad*. He recalled that "I did a page a day for years. Sometimes I could spend a whole day on a panel; other times I could do two pages in a day. It worked out to about a page a day."

Wood scripted two stories that he illustrated for *Weird Fantasy* ("Darkside of the Moon," #15, and "The Enemies of the Colony," #8) as well as plotting two other science fiction stories. In addition to his work for EC, Wood drew science fiction stories for Avon Comics and other companies from 1950 to 1952. Some of this work, like the early EC stories, were drawn with Harry Harrison. When the two men ended their partnership, Joe Orlando joined Wood in his art studio.

Orlando recalled that "we started working together as a team because he liked my

Weird Science #22 © 1953 William M. Gaines. Art by Wally Wood.

drawing and I was knocked out by his inking. He would never do a finished drawing—he would just ink his layouts and it came out looking like the greatest finished art I had seen."

In the spring of 1951, Wood mentioned to Orlando that EC was looking for new artists. "Since they loved his work so much," Orlando recalled, "they were looking for another Wally Wood. Since I was already working with him, I just used his approach and did up a set of samples."

Editor Al Feldstein officially dubbed Orlando "another Wally Wood" and he made his EC science fiction debut in the September 1951 issues of both *Weird Science* and *Weird Fantasy*. "From that point on I was a regular artist," Orlando recalled, "getting a job of six or seven pages every two weeks. We were making about $25 a page, which was pretty good money at the time."

In 1952, Wood introduced another artist to the EC science fiction lineup: his classmate from art school, Al Williamson.

In 1941, Williamson was ten years old when he knew he wanted to be a science fiction comic artist. He had just seen the movie serial *Flash Gordon Conquers the Universe* and the world of science fiction opened up for a young boy. Williamson recalled that after he saw Flash Gordon on the screen, he "looked up the strip and realized how good the drawing was, and how much I liked looking at the pictures, especially the figure work. *Flash Gordon* is the reason I became an artist—Alex Raymond's drawing. But first and

Weird Fantasy #15 © 1952 William M. Gaines. Art by Joe Orlando.

IT WAS AN OLD SHIP! ITS OUTSIDE HULL NO LONGER GLEAMED BRIGHT AND DAZZLING! THE SURFACE WAS PITTED AND POCK-MARKED WITH THE BATTLE SCARS OF COUNTLESS FLIGHTS THROUGH THE ASTEROID BELT! INSIDE ITS TIME-WORN CONTROL COMPARTMENT, ITS COMMANDER, MARTIN KREEGER, CURSED AND SPAT UPON THE PAINT-PEELED FLOOR...

BLASTED GYRO-CONTROL! IT'S ON THE FRITZ AGAIN!

SHALL I GET BELLMAN UP HERE, SIR? WE'VE GOT A CHANGE-OF-COURSE COMING UP IN SIX HOURS foremost the fact that he was my hero."

Williamson came to New York as a teenager and met his idol, Alex Raymond. Through Burne Hogarth's school, he became friends with Roy Krenkel and met artists like George Evans and Frank Frazetta. From late 1949 to 1951, Williamson assisted and worked with Evans, Frazetta, Wood, and Krenkel. After some early work on western comics (*John Wayne*, *Billy the Kid*), he was drawing more and more science fiction by 1951.

Krenkel remembered that Williamson "did almost nothing but science fiction at the time, and that's the only thing I did, what with doing funny cities and crazy machinery stuff like that. And Al was then primarily a figure man. He could do the figures and action, which I couldn't do at all. I, on the other hand, had the background and patience where I enjoyed filling in the holes with funny machinery and buildings and landscapes and things like that, so it was a very happy situation."

Williamson recalled that Krenkel introduced him to the EC science fiction comics: "He told me how good they were, and so I started buying them. I already knew about Wally Wood's work through the Avon comics and I'd met Wally at the school before." Wood eventually convinced Williamson to do a sample page of science fiction to show EC. He was hired on the spot.

From 1952 to 1955, Williamson drew two dozen science fiction stories for EC, occasionally assisting and being assisted by Roy Krenkel and Frank Frazetta.

Weird Science #22 © 1953 William M. Gaines. Art by Wally Wood. From "My World."

Weird Science #16 © 1952 *William M. Gaines.* Art by Al Williamson.

Williamson recalled that "Frank [Frazetta] and Roy [Krenkel] were good friends. And I enjoyed drawing figures very much. Frank inked roughly two or three jobs for me, and I pencilled them. Roy Krenkel pencilled the backgrounds and I inked those. One of the main reasons that I worked with them was that we had a hell of a lot of fun. We'd get together and we'd enjoy working on the stories. We had a a lot of fun, creating a panel, drawing a figure, putting a figure in a Roy Krenkel background, and, you know, creating something together. We enjoyed it very much and it was a very happy time."

Roy Krenkel agreed. "It was a different world. It wasn't a matter of the money, it was

*Weird Fantasy #14 ©
1952 William M.
Gaines.* Art by Al
Williamson, Frank
Frazetta, Roy Krenkel.

frankly, we worked mostly for each other . . . it felt good to be noticed."

Joe Orlando recalled that "for the first time, we were working with intelligent people putting out intelligent products. They really cared about what they were doing. They had a high regard for their writers and artists—the atmosphere was unique."

As Roy Krenkel said, it was "just the right particular guys happened to be working at the right particular time for the right particular company. And we enjoyed the stuff at the time. It wasn't work. Every damn last one of us had the feeling that, 'You know, at times I can't believe I'm getting paid for this stuff.'"

It proved too good to last. Although never as popular as horror comics, science fiction comics at least were profitable. But by late 1952, EC's science fiction comics were no longer showing a healthy profit. Gaines recalled, "we were actually losing money on them, and we published them merely because we loved them." By the end of 1953, however, Gaines had to combine his two science fiction comics into one title, *Weird Science-Fantasy* (March 1954), in order to save money. The high quality of art and stories

the love of the stuff. We got a bang out of it. I mean we'd leap up in the middle of drawing. I well remember this. I was with Al [Williamson] and Woody [Wally Wood] one day, and all of a sudden Woody would jump out of his chair—same with Al and the same with me—and go, 'Hey look! Look at this idea! Look at this arrangement of panels! Follow this sequence! Get the action! I particularly like this figure, you know?' Right in the middle of work we'd be talking art rather than making a buck, and we were all full of enthusiasm."

Frank Frazetta remembered the circle of EC artists as "sort of a mutual admiration society . . . a lot of fun, a lot of flattery. Compliments if you do a good job. And

*Incredible Science Fiction #30 © 1955 William M.
Gaines.* Art by Jack Davis.

IT IS A WORLD OF EXPLORATION INTO THE UNKNOWN... THE SUDDEN THRILL OF GAZING UPON AN ALIEN LANDSCAPE THAT NO HUMAN BEING HAS EVER GAZED UPON BEFORE...

Weird Science #22 © 1953 William M. Gaines. Art by Wally Wood.

remained the same as before, but science fiction comics in general were no longer selling like they had two, even three years earlier.

EC's horror comics, however, were still selling well in 1954, despite the increasing criticism leveled against horror and crime comics by social critics and parents. In October 1954, the comic book industry attempted to combat the bad publicity the horror and crime comics were generating. They established a Comics Code to eliminate what some critics had called objectionable material in comic books produced for children. The words "horror" and "terror" could no longer be used in the title of a comic book.

Some newsstand distributors and operators, in the backlash suffered by the horror comics, did not even want the word "weird" in a comic book title. Gaines had been forced to drop his horror comics, and now he changed the name of *Weird Science-Fantasy* to *Incredible Science Fiction* (July 1955) to gain newsstand acceptance.

Gaines also submitted *Incredible Science Fiction* for review and approval by the Comics Code Authority in order to get newsstand distribution. He became immediately frustrated by their attempts to sanitize the stories and remove anything even remotely daring or objectionable. When the Comics Code vetoed an anti-bigotry story in *Incredible Science Fiction* #33 (February 1956) on the grounds that the main character—a black man—was shown sweating, Gaines decided it was time to leave the comic book business. He put all his energies into *Mad* magazine, and so ended a grand era in science fiction comics.

The EC writers and artists, however, left a rich legacy and a host of imitators in their place. Not only did the EC comics bring a new type of science fiction to comic book readers, they also helped spark a boom in other science fiction comics during the early 1950s.

Soon, there was enough weird science and weird fantasy in the early 1950s to fill a newsstand rack full of comic books.

FLYING SAUCERS AND STRANGE ADVENTURES

In the summer of 1947, the Flying Saucers came. Kenneth Arnold was piloting his plane over the night skies of Washington State in June that year when he noticed a group of strange objects in the sky. He could not identify them, but reported that they were shaped like saucers. In July, Arnold again reported the flying objects. Newspapers around the country quickly dubbed them "flying saucers."

Weird Science #13 © 1950 William M. Gaines. Art by Al Feldstein.

Throughout the late 1940s, hundreds of people reported seeing "flying saucers." Was Earth being invaded? Was the military testing a new weapon? And we asked both fearfully and hopefully: Were They Real?

In a magazine published in 1950, a psychiatrist stated: "The flying saucers are mass hysteria brought about by postwar insecurity and economic anxiety. It is obviously a pathological illusion brought about by continuous publicity given to it by press, radio, and *comic books*."

The magazine, it should be carefully noted, was a comic book—*Weird Science* #13 (July 1950)—and the psychiatrist was a comic book character in a story created by William Gaines and Al Feldstein.

The story, "Flying Saucer Invasion," was an obvious jab at the establishment. Gaines recalled that "Al and I were about 75% convinced that there were such things as flying saucers. We sure hoped that there were . . . just the whole idea that the Air Force was sup-

pressing something was delightful anyway. So even if it weren't true, we wished it were."

A lot of people were intrigued by the saucer sightings. The first major book about them, *Flying Saucers Are Real*, appeared in 1950 by Donald Keyhoe, a prominent UFO investigator. Kenneth Arnold, the man who saw the first "saucers" in 1947, told his story in *The Coming of the Saucers* (1952).

The 1951 movie *The Day the Earth Stood Still*, with a flying saucer landing on the White House lawn, played to a popular fear that only a Force from the Outside could save Earth from atomic doom. Flying saucers and their occupants were also hailed as mankind's saviors in George Adamski's popular book *Flying Saucers Have Landed* (1953).

On the other hand, flying saucers were also viewed with suspicion and paranoia. What if the aliens weren't friendly and they used their super-scientific weapons of destruction upon us, as they gleefully did in the 1956 movie *Earth Versus The Flying Saucers*?

Facing page: *Venus #10 © 1950 Marvel Entertainment Group, Inc.*

Vic Torry and His Flying Saucer #1 © 1950 Fawcett Publications. Art by Bob Powell.

In late 1954, EC published a special flying saucer issue of *Weird Science-Fantasy* (#26, December 1954). Unlike other flying saucer comics, however, these stories were not mere fiction: "E.C. Challenges the U.S. Air Force with this illustrated, factual FLYING SAUCER REPORT!"

Publisher William Gaines remembered that "Donald Keyhoe was the basis of this; he had written a couple of books and a few articles on it. And we called him up and invited him to New York. He spent a whole day with us, and Al [Feldstein] either taped it or took copious notes." Feldstein then wrote the comic book using actual dates, names,

and quotes from Keyhoe's investigations and reports.

The comic book received an enormous amount of publicity. Gaines recalled that "Frank Edwards, a radio commentator of the time who did believe in flying saucers and who wrote a best-selling book on the subject, gave us a lot of publicity on his radio show which resulted in thousands and thousands of mail orders of the dime book. We were inundated."

The strong visual imagery of flying saucers was perfect for the comic books. Other comic publishers besides EC also capitalized on the flying saucer boom. Avon Comics published an issue of *Flying Saucers* (1950), drawn by Wally Wood in his early EC days. Fawcett Publishing entered the science fiction arena with *Vic Torry and His Flying Saucer* (1950), as drawn by Bob Powell.

Flying saucers, however, were just the most visible tip of a growing public fascination for the fantastic and for science fiction in all its forms—literature, comics, radio, movies, and now the newest medium: television.

Captain Video, the first television science fiction series, began in June 1949. The show was broadcast live five nights a week for nearly five years. Over three million kids watched Captain Video and his Video Rangers battle monsters from space and harness runaway comets, all accomplished with embarrassingly sparse special effects. The popularity of the show spawned a *Captain Video* comic book (February 1951)—the first of many crossovers between science fiction television series and comic books.

In October 1950, *Tom Corbett: Space Cadet* made his TV debut with three 15-minute weekly episodes. Tom, a cadet in the Space Academy of the University of Planets, is training with his fellow space cadets—Alfie, Roger, and Astro—to be interplanetary officers in the Solar Alliance. Their TV adventures inspired a 1951 newspaper comic strip and a *Tom Corbett* comic book (January 1952). Like the TV show, the comic book was full of juvenile jostling and jiving, like a 1930s prep school football team:

"Hey, you spacelugs," says Astro to his fellow cadets. "This code message sounds tougher than Plutonian granite!"

"Give it to me, you Venusian swamp lizard," his teammate says. "This should be real easy for *me!*"

"Stop acting like a spacenut! This message may be serious," says Tom.

"It's going to be plenty serious—when I knock this Venusian swamp monkey for a spaceloop!"

"Get out of the way, Tom! I can take care of this noisy bag of space gas!"

While TV and comics captured the juvenile audience, dozens of science fiction magazines at the newsstands took aim at teenage and adult readers. In 1950, a new science fiction magazine was launched almost every month: *The Magazine of Fantasy and Science Fiction, Fantastic Story Quarterly, Fantasy Fiction, Future Science Fiction, Out of This World Adventures, Galaxy Science Fiction, Imagination, Marvel Science Stories*, and *Worlds Beyond*. A new generation of readers discovered a new breed of writers in the digest-size science fiction magazines of the 1950s.

Science fiction's biggest impact on the general public in 1950, however, came from a single movie: *Destination Moon*. Based on

Tom Corbett, Space Cadet #11 © 1954 Videofeatures Co.

Weird Science-Fantasy #26 © 1954 William M. Gaines. Art by Al Feldstein.

Robert Heinlein's novel *Rocketship Galileo* (1947), *Destination Moon* was the first major science fiction movie since *Things To Come* in 1936. Produced for the then-lavish cost of $586,000 by George Pal (who used puppetoon animation techniques and space paintings by Chesley Bonestell to achieve a "you-are-there-documentary" look), the movie heralded the beginning of a boom in 1950s science fiction movies. A comic book adaptation of *Destination Moon* was also released as part of the *Fawcett Movie Comic* series in 1950.

That same year, *Rocketship X-M* (a $95,000 "quickie") was rushed to the screens to exploit the new interest in science fiction. The following year saw the release of three classic movies: *When Worlds Collide*, *The Day the Earth Stood Still*, and *The Thing* (based on John Campbell's story "Who Goes There"). Dozens of more science fiction movies appeared in the early 1950s, ranging from the sublime (*War of the Worlds*, *Forbidden Planet*) to the ridiculous (*Robot Monster*, *Abbott & Costello Go to Mars*).

Along with the new movies, television shows, and science fiction magazines, there were also dozens of new science fiction comic books introduced in late 1950 and 1951. Some were drawn by the same artists who were working on the EC science fiction comics.

During his early EC comics career, Wally Wood worked for Avon Comics, as did his

Captain Science #4 ©
1951 Youthful Magazines.
Art by Joe Orlando and
Wally Wood.

ON A COLD, DISMAL NIGHT IN MARCH, 1951, A WHITE HOT BALL OF FIRE HURTLES FROM THE SKY OVER NEW MEXICO...

...AND WITH AN EARTH-SHAKING THUD CRASHES INTO THE GROUND OUTSIDE OF CAPTAIN SCIENCE'S SECRET LABORATORY...

ART BY JOE ORLANDO
AND WALLACE WOOD

FROM OUT OF SPACE CAME AN URGENT PLEA FROM THE BEATEN INHABITANTS OF THE PLANET MARS BEGGING CAPTAIN SCIENCE TO HELP THEM, BUT HOW COULD HE, EVEN WITH ALL HIS VAST INTER-PLANETARY KNOWLEDGE AND SCIENTIFIC KNOW-HOW, FREE A WHOLE WORLD FROM THE EVIL AND DEADLY GRIP OF

THE MARTIAN SLAVERS...

> **"What is in store for mankind tomorrow? Will he soon soar away into the limitless reaches of outer space? Four courageous men attempt to answer this thrilling question as they blaze an interplanetary trail, rocketing into the unknown with . . . Destination MOON!"**
>
> — *from* Destination Moon, *the comic book adaptation*

partner, Joe Orlando. In 1951, Wood drew *Earthman on Venus* and Orlando worked on *Rocket to the Moon*. Both men then teamed up to illustrate *Captain Science* for Youthful Comics. In preparation for their later EC science fiction stories, Al Williamson, Frank Frazetta, and Roy Krenkel worked with Orlando and Wood on Avon's science fiction comic *Strange Worlds* (#3, May 1951).

Another appreciated artist who worked on the early 1950s science fiction comics was Basil Wolverton of *Spacehawk* fame. After *Spacehawk* was dropped, Wolverton abandoned science fiction and drew dozens of humorous features like "Powerhouse Pepper," "Bingbang Buster," and "Hash House" from 1942 to 1951. From 1951 to 1953, Wolverton rediscovered science fiction comics ("necessary to keep both my brain cells headed in other directions").

He wrote and drew eight bizarre science fiction stories, including "The End of the World," "Planet of Terror," "The Monster on Mars," and "The Brain Bats of Venus" for comic books like *Weird Tales of the Future* and *Journey Into Unknown Worlds*. In what Wolverton described as his favorite story from that period, "Eye of Doom," a crew of returning space explorers brings back a hideous alien life form from Venus, a gigantic eyeball that devours and assimilates humans and animals.

"I've had what appeared to be normal adults," Wolverton recalled, "tell me to my face that they wouldn't allow their offspring to as much glance at the horrible looking faces I draw."

Not all the early 1950s science fiction comics were as scary as Wolverton's stories. Many were strictly from the "flying saucers and tasty dishes" school of bug-eyed monsters and gossamer-wrapped space queens. The tradition of *Planet Comics* was proudly carried on in such comics as *Amazing Adventures*, *Space Action*, and *Space Adventures*—home of Rex Clive, Space Officer:

"The Space Officers! Their purpose: to patrol the planets in the year 2552. In their uniforms of stratosphere blue, they stand for law and order from Mercury to Pluto and even beyond the limits of our solar system!"

In the story "The Vixens of Venus" (*Space Adventures* #3, November 1952), Rex Clive and his fellow space officer Speed Lancing are knocked unconscious by the fumes of opium poppies from Venus. They are kidnapped and

Weird Tales Of The Future #5 © 1953 Stanley P. Morse/Aragon Publishing. Art by Basil Wolverton from "The Man From the Moon."

Space Action #3 © 1952 Junior Books, Inc.

transported to Venus by a crew of women who deliver the men to their queen Delva:

"One pair of Earthian apes for the Royal Insectarium!"

The nonplussed Rex shrugs off the insult: "Looks like the Queen Bee of this Venus crowd—the chief vixen herself!"

With the help of Stella Dawn of the Woman's Space Officer Auxiliary, the two men escape from the vixens and their giant pet spiders and pink Venusian worms.

Occasionally, however, the stories would rise above juvenile space opera, such as "Transformation," drawn by Dick Giordano for *Space*

Rocket to the Moon #1 © 1951 Avon Periodicals, Inc. Art by Joe Orlando.

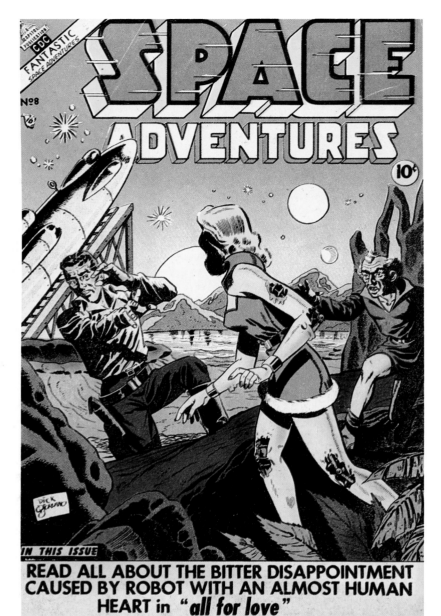

Space Adventures #8 © 1953 Charlton Comics. Art by Dick Giordano.

Space Adventures #7 © 1953 Charlton Comics. Art by Dick Giordano.

Adventures #7 (July 1953):

Nuclear war threatens the earth. A medical researcher decides to lead a group of scientists to a new planet. His fiancée, Betty, goes with him on the rocket ship.

The rocket crashes on a planet, however, and all of the scientists are killed—except the doctor and Betty. The woman wakes up from the crash, without her memory, and wanders dazedly away. When the doctor regains consciousness, he believes that he is the only survivor.

As the months go by, the doctor constructs a laboratory from the rocket's wreckage: "I'll go nuts by myself here if I'm not careful! I'll try working in the lab."

Meanwhile, Betty slowly regains her memory but is unable to find the wreckage of the rocket or the doctor. As for Betty's boyfriend, the story reminds us: "Months of loneliness can produce strange fixations in the most brilliant minds . . . "

The doctor speculates: "These notes on sex conversion . . . the transformation from male to female of the human being by medical science might provide an interesting experiment. Take a long time to accomplish, but I've got a lot of time! Anyway, I'm a little tired of being a man . . . men start wars and build rockets to escape from them. Men would, in short, seem to be rather stupid creatures. This hormone shot will start the treatment . . . "

Meanwhile, Betty is now searching for the doctor and any other survivors. She stumbles across the wreckage of the rocket and her fiancee's laboratory. Then she sees another woman: "Who the devil are you? I was the only woman on board! Where is Dr. Kranston?"

The other woman sobs: "Betty . . . I'm Dr. Kranston! I've undergone a transformation of sex by my own hand! The others . . . all dead. We're the last alive. But . . . but Betty . . . I didn't know . . . "

Betty sees the changed contours under the shirt of her former fiancé and then realizes: "Transformation . . . oh, no . . . "

After sex, drugs could not be far behind. Rod Hathaway, Space Detective, took on the "Opium Smugglers of Venus" in *Space Detective* (July 1951). Drawn by Wally Wood, the story features a hard-boiled gumshoe, his girl Friday, a drug-addicted actress, and a murderous Martian. Rod breaks up the interplanetary dope ring when he discovers a field of poppies and a narcotics factory hidden in the jungles of Venus.

Science fiction was so popular in the early 1950s that not only were detectives shot off into outer space, but so were cowboys. In 1952, Charlton Comics changed its comic *Cowboy Western*, which featured Jesse James and Annie Oakley, into a futuristic-hybrid called *Space Western* (October 1952). Spurs Jackson and his Space Vigilantes fought Martians and Nazis on the moon when they weren't roping cattle on their Bar-Z Ranch in

Arizona. When a flying saucer lands in his cattle corral, a nonchalant Spurs ambles up to the alien: "Well, well! Don't tell me you're from Mars!"

The Martians capture Spurs and his range rowdies, but the aliens don't know that the cowboy packs a six-gun which fires "miniature atomic bombs." Spur and his cowboys, however, use a conventional lariat and bullwhip to send the saucer boys packing.

Although some comic book writers and editors in the early 1950s regarded science fiction as just another marketable genre, like westerns, romance, or horror, there were others who came to the field with knowledgeable experience and an impressive background, such as DC Comics' editor Julius Schwartz.

Schwartz read his first issue of *Amazing Stories* in the late 1920s and, by admission, "was hooked" forever on science fiction. At the age of 16, he helped launch the first widely distributed science fiction fan magazine, *The Time Traveller* (January 1932). In 1934, along with fellow fan Mort Weisinger, Schwartz started the first science fiction literary agency, "Solar Sales." His clients soon included Edmond Hamilton, Henry Kuttner,

Space Western #40 © 1952 Charlton Comics. Art by John Belfi.

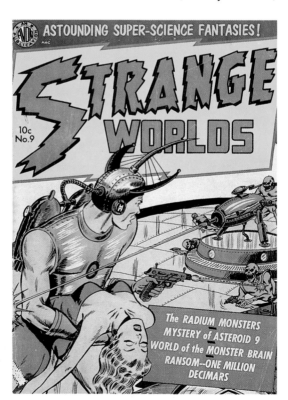

Strange Worlds #9 © 1952 Avon Periodicals, Inc.

Robert Bloch, H. P. Lovecraft, and Alfred Bester.

In 1944, Bester, who was now writing comic book scripts for *Green Lantern* comics, referred Schwartz to an editorial opening in the All-American Comic Group (later part of DC Comics). Schwartz was promptly hired and put to work editing *Flash*, *Green Lantern*, *All-Star Comics*, and other costumed hero comics. By 1950, many of these titles were canceled as sales of superhero comics fell.

Science fiction, however, was capturing the public's imagination. The movie *Destination Moon* provided part of the impetus for DC Comics to launch its first science fiction comic, *Strange Adventures* (August 1950). The first issue naturally featured an adaptation of the movie. The editor for the new comic was also a natural choice: Julius Schwartz.

When Schwartz began *Strange Adventures*, he looked for writers who had experience in the field—authors he had worked with and represented in the past. And, unlike most comic books of the time, the writers were given a byline in the magazine. Schwartz even put their names on the covers for the early issues and sometimes had their likenesses drawn into the comic stories.

"When I did *Strange Adventures*," Schwartz recalled, "I gave credits, especially because I used big-time science fiction writers. I used Edmond Hamilton; H. L. Gold, who was later

Strange Adventures #6
© 1951 DC Comics, Inc.

Strange Adventures #8 © 1951 DC Comics, Inc.

the editor and founder of *Galaxy Science Fiction*; Manly Wade Wellman, who was a grand master of science fiction and fantasy. I thought it would have name value. Someone who reads science fiction would see the name Edmond Hamilton and would pick it up."

Evidently, enough readers picked up *Strange Adventures* for Schwartz to launch a companion science fiction comic, *Mystery In Space*. Schwartz used many of the same writers who worked on *Strange Adventures*, including Leigh Brackett, Otto Binder, Gardner Fox, Ed Herron, John Broome, David V. Reed, and Sam Merwin, the former editor of *Thrilling Wonder Stories* and *Startling Stories*.

Unlike the cynical and wry EC science fiction comics, the stories in DC Comics's *Strange Adventures* and *Mystery in Space* were usually brightly optimistic with upbeat endings.

In a typical *Strange Adventures* story "Do Not Open Till Doomsday!" (#36, September 1953), strange objects from outer space fall all over the Earth. A government scientist suspects that the objects, disguised as gifts, are actually "secret weapons designed to soften up this planet for an interplanetary invasion!"

To confirm his theory, a fleet of space-ships suddenly appears from outer space. As the nations of Earth prepare to launch an H-Bomb attack, the spaceships spell out birthday greetings in all the languages of the world.

The government scientist calls off the attack: "I should have guessed earlier the meaning of the 'gifts'! The Earth was born exactly 4 billion years ago *this* year! Our neighboring planets sent us those objects as—*birthday presents*! Happy Birthday to the Earth! Now—let's go out and welcome the people of other planets as—*friends*!"

Many of the DC science fiction stories were often cleverly plotted mysteries with fantastic settings or punchlines. There was always a protagonist who solved the problem, saved the world, or halted the alien invasion through a clever application of scientific reasoning and good, old-fashioned courage. Like the EC science fiction comics, however, there was also social satire in some of the stories, however mild and gentle.

For example, the story "It's a Woman's World!" (*Mystery In Space* #8, July 1952), written by John Broome, made an interesting

Mystery in Space #38 © 1957 DC Comics, Inc.

Mystery in Space #19 © 1954 DC Comics, Inc. Art by Virgil Finlay.

statement on sexual discrimination and gender roles:

In 2980 the first woman was selected president of the Earth federation. By 3100 women had replaced men in key positions in all walks of life. The pilots of Earth's war-rockets which conquered the galaxy in the 33rd century were—women. In sports, women played—while puny men watched and applauded. To men passed the roles of domestics and housekeepers. . . .

The hero of our story, a teenage boy named Greg, vacuums the house while his mother prepares for her job as a rocket pilot.

*Mystery in Space #1 ©
1951 DC Comics, Inc.
Art by Frank Frazetta.*

man and the two decide to marry.

Greg tells his new bride: "In *our* house, Stella—vacuuming will be *your* job!" She replies: "Yes dear! Whatever you say!"

"I was the first, Stella," Greg tells his wife, "but now more and more young men are becoming rocket cadets—and leaders everywhere!"

"We women ran things long enough, Greg," Stella sighs, "it's time you men took over again!"

The women, however, were still in charge in another DC science fiction series. Astra, Girl of the Future, appeared in *Sensation Comics* (October 1950), along with Wonder Woman, and in other female-oriented series like "Romance, Inc." and "Dr. Pat."

Created by writer and editor Robert Kanigher, Astra is a telecaster for Transvideo News, an interplanetary reporter of the future. When an alien "strangler tree" attacks her traveling companion, Professor Rockwell, Astra "cooly, swiftly whips out her electro-pistol" and blasts the tree tentacle away from the man's head. "Good shot, Astra," he says. "I couldn't afford to *miss*, professor," she crisply replies.

Quick-thinking, poised, and independent, Astra was a welcome role model in the pantheon of space babes and bubbleheads who inhabited the other science fiction comics and pulp magazines.

Another early science fiction series created by Robert Kanigher, "Knights of the Galaxy," appeared in the first several issues of *Mystery In Space* (April 1951–June 1952). For

"But mother," he asks, "why can't I go to rocket cadet school like you did?"

"Because you're a man, Greg—that's why!"

Greg persists, however, and becomes the first man in recent history to enter rocket cadet school. ("Somehow I feel I must succeed—and prove that a man can do anything a girl can!")

The female instructors at school reluctantly send Greg out on a training mission. "We'll have to send him on a mission—but of course he'll only be a nuisance in the actual fighting!" The other teacher agrees: "Of course! Men can't fight!"

Under battle fire, however, Greg proves himself and rescues Captain Stella, his female commander. She falls in love with the brave

Mystery in Space #8 © 1952 DC Comics, Inc. Art by Bob Oksner.

Strange Adventures #3 © 1950 DC Comics, Inc.

its companion title *Strange Adventures*, Edmond Hamilton created a series called "The Adventures of Chris KL-99."

Chris KL-99 was the first human being born in space. Together with his two crew members, a Venusian scientist named Jero and a Martian adventurer named Halk, he explores the stars in his spaceship, the Pioneer. As the discoverer of so many new worlds, Chris was often referred to as the "Columbus of Space."

The series lasted for a little more than a year and was drawn by Murphy Anderson, an artist already recognized for his talent in the science fiction field. Anderson, who had drawn the Star Pirate series for *Planet Comics* from 1944 to 1947, came to DC Comics fresh from his stint as the artist on the "Buck Rogers" daily newspaper strip (1947–1949).

"I always envisioned myself doing a science fiction strip as a career," Anderson recalled. "I had no formal art training, outside of a little art in college, but I loved comic books! I grew up on Will Eisner, Lou Fine, and Reed Crandall later. But *Buck Rogers* was the first big impression. I was simply fascinated by the concept of Buck Rogers, and I made a

great effort to get an out-of-town newspaper every week just to get Buck. I was about ten or eleven years old at the time. I've always loved science fiction."

Anderson illustrated nearly one hundred science fiction stories for DC Comics in the 1950s. For *Strange Adventures*, he drew the majority of the Captain Comet stories from 1951 to 1954, a series created by writer John Broome.

Captain Comet was the first of a long line of scientific superheroes from DC Comics. He wore a red spacesuit uniform, had a secret identity (Adam Blake), and was a mild-mannered librarian. Through a genetic accident, Adam Blake has the mental and physical capabilities of a person born 100,000 years

Mystery in Space #18 © 1954 DC Comics, Inc. Art by Murphy Anderson.

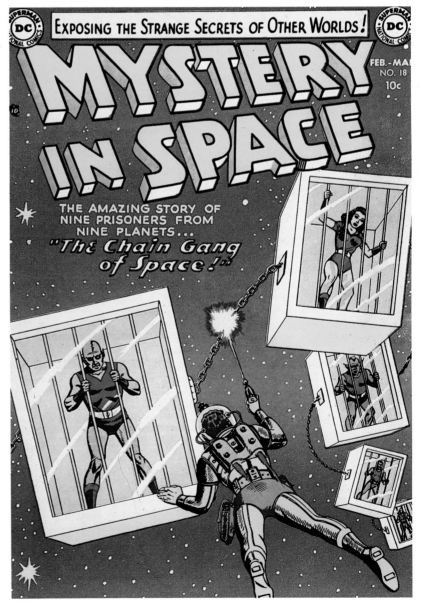

from now—"an accidental specimen of future man." Blake builds his own jetship, the Cometeer, which is powered by an "ultra-spectrum drive."

Although he has such powers as levitation and telepathy, Captain Comet usually relies upon innate cleverness to beat his enemies. When a gang of marauding *invisible* aliens comes after him, he grabs a spray paint gun and outlines their forms. "As long as I can see these creatures, I can hit them with enough concentrated mental energy to paralyze them for awhile!" As his companion and confidant Dr. Zackro gushes, "Comet, there's no end to your ingenuity!"

Another ingenious DC science fiction

*Strange Adventures #22 ©
1952 DC Comics, Inc.* Art
by Murphy Anderson.

Strange Adventures #27 © 1952 DC Comics, Inc. Art by
Murphy Anderson.

character at the time was Tommy Tomorrow, the typical 21st-century teenage space cadet who was training to be an interplanetary policeman. Tommy Tomorrow of the Planeteers made an early appearance in 1946 (*Real Fact Comics* #6) and then received a regular series in the back pages of *Action Comics* from 1948 to 1958, as drawn by Curt Swan and later Jim Mooney. Interestingly enough, Tommy Tomorrow preceded the early 1950s boom in TV teenage space kid shows like *Tom Corbett* and *Space Patrol*.

During the early 1950s, the sales of comic books were reaching an all-time high, with over 500 titles on the newsstands. Science fiction comics had also enjoyed a similar surge in popularity. At the end of 1949, *Planet Comics* was the only regularly published science fiction comic book. In 1950, there were more than a dozen new titles, including EC's *Weird Science* and *Weird Fantasy*. In 1951, the number of science fiction comics published doubled and then increased again the following year.

From 1953 to 1954, however, the number of regularly published science fiction comics dropped to fewer than ten. Flying saucers gradually disappeared from the headlines. Little green men did not appear on the White House lawn. The need for science fiction to help explain the uncertainties of the future was temporarily abated.

Yet, in only a few years, an event would occur that would once again cause us to watch the skies, to wonder fiercely about the future, and to look again to science fiction for a clue about tomorrow.

Weird Tales Of The Future #2 © 1952 Stanley P. Morse/Aragon Publishing. Art by Basil Wolverton.

SPACE RACE ACES AND HEROES

Atomic bombs from outer space became more science than fiction in 1957. Russians launched the first satellite—Sputnik—and beat America off the line in the race for space. Three years earlier, the USSR had exploded its first hydrogen bomb. Science and space technology had suddenly become Very Important.

World Around Us #5 © 1959 Gilberton Publications. Art by Weiker.

The United States began an aggressive space program in 1958 and launched the Explorer I. The next year, the Russians photographed the far side of the moon. Putting a man on the moon became a national priority. Science became a driving force in not only our education but also our entertainment. Science fiction was the literature of the day.

Within weeks after Sputnik became a new word in our vocabulary, a comic book appeared with the most timely title imaginable: *Race for the Moon* (March 1958). Inside were stories of American astronauts and Soviet cosmonauts—three years before the first man was launched into outer space. We wanted to see the future. We wanted to find out who would win the race for the moon.

Besides fictionalized treatments of the space race in comics, there were also comic books that purported to show us the "real" thing—more science than fiction. Classics Illustrated comics presented an 80-page look at *The Illustrated History of Space* (January 1959) which gave kids a look at how the first man-spaced flight would take place, complete with up-to-the-minute specifications

on NASA's Jupiter-C and Vanguard rockets. Walt Disney's *Man in Space* (October 1959) gave the comic book treatment to three Disney educational films on outer-space exploration.

There was a general feeling in the late 1950s that everyone, and especially kids, should learn more about space and science—especially since the Russians had gotten the jump on us.

Murphy Anderson, a longtime science fiction artist who drew the *Buck Rogers* daily strip from 1947 to 1949, returned to the strip again in 1958. He recalled that when Sputnik was launched, "Buck Rogers suddenly became hot again. The syndicate salesman sold the strip to every paper he called on during a trip back from Texas."

Jack Kirby, who drew several stories for *Race for the Moon*, moved on to Marvel Comics in 1958 and brought his interest in science fiction with him. Kirby, whose early comic book work included a 1940 series called "Solar Legion" for *Crash Comics*, was adept at drawing space vehicles and futuristic machinery with detailed realism. One of his first jobs at

Facing page: *Race for the Moon #3* © 1958 Harvey Features Syndicate. Art by Jack Kirby.

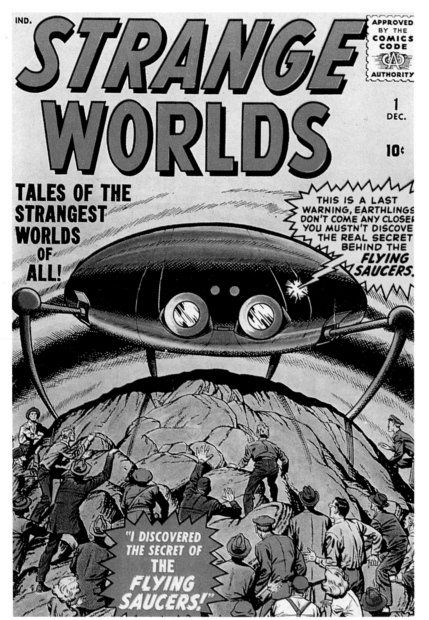

Strange Worlds #1 © 1958 Marvel Entertainment Group, Inc. Art by Jack Kirby.

Marvel Comics in 1958 was drawing the cover and a story for *Strange Worlds* (December 1958)—Marvel's first new science fiction title in over two years. Harkening back to the early 1950s, the first issue was all about flying saucers and also featured art by Steve Ditko.

Ditko was also drawing dozens of science fiction stories for Charlton Comics that year, including its first post-sputnik comic, *Outer Space* (May 1958). The cover of the first issue screamed out: "ATTENTION! This is the most vital subject of our times! Every American . . . Man . . . Woman . . . Child owes it to his country and himself to read this issue!"

The following year, Charlton Comics published a title which played upon the big

fear behind our race into space: *Space War* (October 1959). Many of the stories involved alien invasions or futuristic armadas clashing between stars—metaphors perhaps for Cold War anxieties about the space race.

In the story "The Ray of Hate" (*Outer Space #5*, June 1960), such anxieties and growing tensions between world powers were revealed to be part of a master alien invasion plan. The story begins:

> Ever since the rise of Hitler and then through World War II and the following years, there was no peace in the world. Small wars broke out in Indo-China, Korea, Algiers. Many reasons were given: people suddenly wanted new governments, others refused to be colonies of major powers anymore. Aside from wars, there was increasing disregard for law throughout the world. Even craftsmanship waned and shoddy work in produced goods became evident. Distrust! Greed! Hate! It was appearing on too many faces, in too many hearts! But that's how things were planned . . .

We learn, furthermore, that "during the years after World War II, another phenomenon was observed—Unidentified Flying Objects, called saucers because of their shape. These mysterious objects were reported seen over all areas of the globe! The world powers told their peoples they could not explain the saucers, and the governments suspected each other of having the secret craft!"

As the story unfolds, we learn, from an advance guard of an alien invasion who has turned traitor, that the flying saucers did serve a secret purpose: "The flying saucers, as you call them, have hovered over your lands for years, contaminating your minds with hate from the Ray of Hate which has induced distrust and suspicion among you and have divided and weakened your peoples!"

The alerted Earthlings cooperate with the alien informant, and they use the Ray of Hate on the invading flying saucers. "Maddened with distrust and hate among themselves, they began fighting and destroying each other. . . . "

Hate conquers all, so to speak, and with the flying saucers eliminated, "it was the beginning of a great new age of peace."

Comic books in the late 1950s often used science fiction to make a positive statement about an uncertain future. The stories were written for a young and idealistic audience which was looking for heroic role models in the new age of space.

DC Comics, the publisher of *Superman* and *Batman*, was experienced in comic book heroes and science fiction. At an editorial meeting in early 1958, Julius Schwartz recalled that "it was decided to do a scientific hero, as contrasted with the anthology stories in *Strange Adventures* and *Mystery in Space*."

Not only one hero, it turned out, but two science fiction heroes, were proposed. Schwartz remembered discussing the characters with Jack Schiff, the editor of *Tales of the Unexpected*, DC's other science fiction title: "We each had a choice of taking a scientific hero from today or from the future. Jack opted for one from the future. I opted for one from today because I think it's more dramatic having something strange and imaginary hap-

Showcase #17 © 1958 DC Comics, Inc. Art by Gil Kane. Adam Strange.

Tales of the Unexpected #43 © 1959 DC Comics, Inc. Art by Bob Brown. Space Ranger.

pening today than in the far future which is *already* imaginary."

Schwartz's scientific hero "from today" was Adam Strange, while Schiff's hero from the future was the Space Ranger. Both characters made their debut in *Showcase*, DC Comics's tryout title, in 1958. Resulting sales earned Adam Strange a niche in Schwartz's *Mystery In Space* (#53, August 1959), while the Space Ranger began his series the same month in Schiff's *Tales of the Unexpected* (#40, August 1959).

"The Space Ranger," written by Arnold Drake and drawn by Bob Brown, was straight from the classic 1930s spacemen mold: "Out beyond the planet Mars, on one of the thousands of asteroids, a section of rock slides back to reveal the secret hideout of Space Ranger, Guardian of the Solar System!"

Rick Starr, in his secret identity as Space Ranger, flies in his spaceship, the Solar King, and packs an "electron displacer" raygun. He has an efficient, blonde girlfriend named Myra and a pot-bellied pink Plutonian sidekick named Cyrll, who has the ability to change into any interplanetary animal ("I don't know if I can help, but I'll try—as a Venusian Flame Bear!").

Although the Space Ranger blasted and barreled through such rip-roaring adventures as "Invasion of the Jewel-Men," "The Jungle Beasts of Jupiter," and "The Alien Brat from Planet Byra," he also used his brains and wits

Showcase #15 © 1958 DC Comics, Inc. Art by Bob Brown. Space Ranger.

Tales of the Unexpected #56 © 1960 DC Comics, Inc. Art by Bob Brown.

to solve a problem. "Lightning follows a path of ionized air—so by changing the dials of my multi-ray gun to ionize a channel for it to follow, I can divert it away from me!"

While the Space Ranger often made cursory use of scientific facts to beat his enemy, the other 1950s DC space hero, Adam Strange, was a true scientist-hero.

While exploring South American ruins, archaeologist Adam Strange encounters a mysterious "Zeta-Beam" which was directed toward Earth from the planet Rann of the star system Alpha Centauri. The beam teleports the Earth scientist to the city of Rangager on the planet Rann where he meets the scientist Sardath and Alanna, his beautiful daughter.

Adam and Alanna join forces with Sardath to defeat the alien invaders known as the Eternals. Although he has no superpowers, the Earth scientist is given a jet belt to allow him to fly, and other handy Rannian gadgets as well. His cleverness and scientific reasoning, however, prove to be his real strengths on the planet Rann, and he wins the heart of Alanna. Just as things are getting cozy, however, the effects of the Zeta-Beam wear off and

Adam disappears back to Earth.

Fortunately, the Earth passed through the path of the Zeta-Beam at regular intervals and Adam was always able to catch a ride back to Rann for periodic interludes with his girlfriend.

Written by Gardner Fox and drawn by Carmine Infantino for Julius Schwartz's *Mystery In Space* (August 1958), the adventures of Adam Strange appeared for over seven years. Fox, who read all of the Edgar Rice Burroughs novels as a youngster in the 1920s, borrowed elements from Burroughs's John Carter of Mars interplanetary romances and freshened them up with a strong science slant.

"I had always done my own scientific research on Adam Strange," Fox recalled years later. "I had two filing cabinets full of info, as well as part of the attic."

When Adam Strange examines Alanna's uniform for a clue as to how to destroy a radioactive robot, he discovers:

> Ah—the dress is marked with an infinitesimal amount of cosmic radiation! The same radiation that changed

Mystery in Space #75 © 1962 DC Comics, Inc. Art by Carmine Infantino. Adam Strange and Alanna.

the original Zeta-Beam into a teleportational beam! The uniform itself is harmless since it was protected inside a container! But the container absorbed the full force of the radiation and—changed in some manner. It became radioactive, of a sort. Radioactivity decays in time and is measured in half-lives. By bombarding the robot with Alpha particles, we ought to hasten that decaying process—making its atoms lose their own Alpha particles in hurry-up time!

Editor Julius Schwartz remembered that

Adam Strange always was based

Mystery in Space #65 © 1961 DC Comics, Inc. Art by Carmine Infantino.

*Mystery in Space #90 ©
1964 DC Comics, Inc. Art
by Carmine Infantino.*

drew over 150 stories in the 1950s for almost every issue of *Mystery In Space* and *Strange Adventures*, including series like "Interplanetary Insurance" and "Space Museum."

Murphy Anderson inked Infantino's artwork on most of the Adam Strange stories and he was also responsible for designing the original costume. The similarities between Adam Strange's space uniform and Buck Rogers's costume was not entirely coincidental; after all, Anderson was drawing the daily Buck Rogers newspaper strip at about the same time in 1958.

The combination of Infantino, Anderson, and Fox made "Adam Strange" one of the most popular DC adventure series of the late 1950s. With the success of "Space Ranger" and "Adam Strange," other DC science fiction series soon followed.

The Star Rovers, a group of three dilettante adventurers, made their debut in *Mystery In Space* (December 1960). Composed of Rick Purvis (playboy and athlete), Karel Sorensen (former Miss Solar System and adventuress), and Homer Glint (space explorer and novelist-sportsman), the Star Rovers were a "space-jet set" who delighted in dallying with dangerous alien life-forms and solving interplanetary mysteries. Drawn by Sid Greene, the series was written by Gardner Fox, who recalled that he had to contrive stories so that each character "would come up with his own solution to a problem, but then they had to put them all together to discover the real one."

For *Strange Adventures*, Fox created two other series. "The Space Museum" began in May 1959 and was drawn by Carmine Infantino. The concept was simple yet open-ended: A father told his son (and the readers) the stories behind the various alien and space artifacts on display in an Earth museum of the future.

Fox's other series for *Strange Adventures* featured Star Hawkins, a bumbling detective of the future, and his brainy robot secretary, Ilda. "Star Hawkins, 21st-century private eye, complimented himself on having the best secretary on Earth! The fact that Ilda was a robot had a special advantage . . . whenever Star ran short of funds (which he often did), he'd deposit Ilda in a pawnshop and redeem

on scientific facts. I thought of Adam Strange as the thinking man's superhero. He always came into conflict against superior scientific odds, weaponry and so on. All he had going for him was his mind. I always had to figure out how Adam Strange using his scientific knowledge would overcome superior scientific weapons.

Besides the cleverly plotted stories, Carmine Infantino's sleek artwork made Adam Strange one of the most memorable DC science fiction series of all time. Infantino, along with Murphy Anderson, was one of DC Comics's most prolific science fiction artists. He her when fortune smiled his way."

The Star Hawkins stories usually revolved around the mechanical Ilda saving her somewhat incompetent boss with all the loyalty and aplomb of the best Girl Friday. Drawn by Mike Sekowsky and later by Gil Kane, the series presented a wry and lighthearted view of the future.

The third regular series in *Strange Adventures*, however, presented a much darker view of tomorrow. Written by John Broome, the Atomic Knights (*Strange Adventures* June 1960) told the story of a band of survivors living on radioactive Earth after the great nuclear war of 1986:

"World War III—the Great Atomic War is over—and in its wake lies an Earth in ruins! Of plant life, there is none! Of animal life, only a small number of *humans* linger on! There is no government, and the prevailing law is *might makes right*!"

As in feudal times, there are marauding gangs who terrorize the countryside. One such gang is led by a small-time dictator called the Black Baron. To fight this postatomic lawlessness, six survivors, consisting of a scientist, an ex-school teacher, his sister, an

Strange Adventures #117
© 1960 DC Comics, Inc.

Strange Adventures #100 © 1959 DC Comics, Inc.

GORILLA MY DREAMS

"I had a science fiction magazine called *Strange Adventures*. It was a monthly magazine and was selling slightly above average. One issue had a fantastic rise in sales—a leap of ten points. What happened? We looked at the cover which showed a gorilla in a cage in a zoo. The people outside the cage were looking at this gorilla, and the gorilla had a slate in his hand and he had written in chalk, 'Please help me, I am the victim of a horrible scientific experiment.' The way I saw it the issue went over well because the gorilla was acting like a human. And every gorilla cover I did from then on was not a *straight* gorilla cover; he was acting like a human. We did a lot of gorilla covers and they always sold well."

— editor Julius Schwartz

Strange Adventures #144
© 1962 DC Comics, Inc.
Art by Murphy
Anderson.

for this early 1960s series. He recalled that he "enjoyed doing the Atomic Knights but as far as effort goes, I was the loser. It took me half again as long to draw as anything else. Each knight had his own suit of armor, and a different personality in the way he looked, the clothes he wore. And they usually fought the menace together! All five or six of them involved in it! And naturally the menace had to outnumber them. I'd have these crazy panels with 15—16 characters! I still enjoyed all of this because John Broome wrote a very good script. I always liked to work off his stuff. But, gee, it was a real backbreaker!"

Anderson's efforts, however, paid off. The Atomic Knights was voted the most popular series by the readers of *Strange Adventures*. And although the stories were all based on the grim premise of fighting for survival in a radioactive world, the Atomic Knights themselves made a hopeful statement. Gobbling down "anti-radiation" pills, the survivors learned to cope and even found time to fall in love.

Another view of life on Earth after the great nuclear war was presented in *Mighty Samson* (July 1964), published by Gold Key

atomic soldier, and two twin brothers band together. To protect themselves from nuclear fallout, they each don a set of medieval armor which has become radioactive-resistant.

These "atomic knights" in armor decide to help right the wrongs that exist in a post-holocaust society. As their leader, Gayle Gardner says: "Humanity needs an organization like ours! There aren't any police—there isn't any government, so far as we know! There is no authority—except evil power—like the Black Baron wielded! Someone has to present law and order and the forces of justice in these terrible times—and it looks like the job is ours! We have to be ready to help people!"

Murphy Anderson drew all fifteen stories

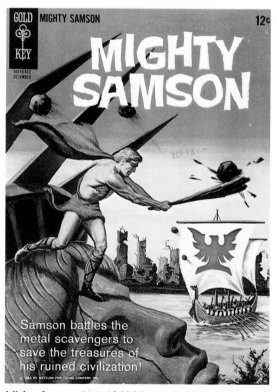

Mighty Samson #4 © 1965 Western Publishing Company, Inc.

Magnus, Robot Fighter #18 © 1967 Western Publishing Company, Inc. Art by Russ Manning. Leeja, 41st-century girlfriend of Magnus Robot Fighter.

comics: "A once-great city lies in ruins, overgrown by a dense jungle. Strange, glowing mists hover ominously, remains of a great nuclear war which devastated the planet. The hopes and dreams of mankind are buried beneath tons of rubble, but in this fantastic world, man himself lives on . . . "

Only small tribes of humans and grotesquely mutated animals roam the earth. Amongst the ruins of New York City (now called N'Yark), beasts like six-pawed gorillas, flying wolves, and liobears (half lions and half bears) roam the streets.

Samson of the N'Yark tribe possesses the strength of ten and uses his powers to fight the monsters. He is befriended by a young woman, Sharmaine, and her father, Mindor, a scientist who has managed to preserve some 20th-century technology and artifacts (like books) in a bank vault. Drawn by Frank Thorne, *Mighty Samson* was a sobering view of one possible future where failed science has caused only destruction and ruin.

Another view of the future and the risks of technology out of control were presented in

Gold Key's *Magnus, Robot Fighter* (February 1963):

It's AD 4000. The North American continent is now one entire multilevel megapolis called North Am. Robots, from police officers (Pol-Robs) to doctors (Medi-Robs), do all the work. Most citizens enjoy a life pampered by robot servants. Others feel, however, that humans have become so dependent that they are losing the ability to defend themselves from renegade or malfunctioning robots.

In this minority group of robot critics and resisters are Leeja Clane, daughter of Senator Clane of North Am, and Magnus, Robot Fighter. Magnus, an orphan, was raised by 1A, a robot mentor with nearly human intelligence.

Magnus, Robot Fighter #5 © 1964 Western Publishing Company, Inc. Art by Russ Manning.

Magnus, Robot Fighter #5 © 1964 Western Publishing Company, Inc. Art by Russ Manning. Magnus Robot Fighter.

Evans, Gene Autry, and *Sea Hunt,* was a long-time science fiction fan and a natural choice to draw the new comic. His polished, clean style seemed perfect for capturing the sleek world of the future. With his science fiction background, Manning was given free reign in designing the character of Magnus and in writing the first issue of the comic book.

Manning made *Magnus, Robot Fighter* one of the best drawn science fiction comic books of the 1960s. The art and concept for the comic worked on several levels. Older readers were fascinated by Manning's vision of a 41st-century society and its technology; younger readers just liked to see Magnus smashing up bad robots (WHANG! SPLANG! SQUEEEEEE!).

Actually, the robots alone would have made Magnus a successful comic. Readers often sent in their own drawings and suggestions for robots to the comic's letter column, *Robot Rostrum:* "This robot is called 'Invinci-Rob' because it is supposed to be invincible. It has every known weapon, blast rays, beams that turn anything to dust, and a force shield. It has a speed twice the speed of thought, and it has a robot army of its own. If you can think

Magnus explains to his girlfriend Leeja that "1A foresaw man's troubles with evil robots, and he trained me to help combat them! He poured knowledge into me, then gave me steel-smashing strength by an incredible training method he perfected."

The idea for *Magnus, Robot Fighter* came from Chase Craig, an editor at Western Publishing (Gold Key Comics). Gold Key had just obtained the rights to publish a comic book based on the futuristic cartoon show, *The Jetsons,* and Craig wanted to publish another comic book based on science fiction concepts. This one, however, had to be strictly serious and it had to have plenty of robots.

Russ Manning, an artist who had worked for Western Publishing on such titles as *Dale*

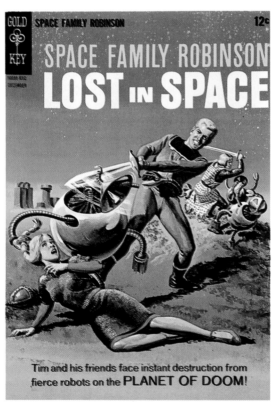

Space Family Robinson #19 © 1966 Western Publishing Company, Inc. Art by George Wilson.

Space War #8 © 1960 Charlton Comics. Art by Steve Ditko.

of a way for Magnus to defeat it, please let me know."

Another successful science fiction comic book from Gold Key was *Space Family Robinson* (December 1962). Walt Disney's *Swiss Family Robinson* was playing in movie theaters the year before editor Del Connell came up with his idea for a comic book about the American space age family:

"TIME . . . The Future.

PLACE . . . The Solar System.

The first family to live in space, the Robinsons—June and Craig and their children Tim and Tam—are threatened with destruction of their space station home by a shower of fiery meteors . . . "

Artist Dan Spiegle, who was drawing cowboy adventures for Dell's *Maverick* comic book, recalled that "at that time, Del Connell, a Western editor, was writing the origin issue for *Space Family Robinson*, and they asked me to draw up a cast of characters. Western liked them so much that they assigned me the strip."

Spiegle was allowed to create his own vision of the future with America's first family in space. "Space Station #1 just progressively evolved out of my imagination. One thing led to another, and I had a fully equipped spaceship with solar gardens, space pods, and the whole works. I fashioned the space pods, by the way, out of my electric razor. The only law that was set before me concerning the design was that I was not to make the space station look like one of those round uninteresting satellites—the type that satellites are 'supposed' to look like."

Mom and dad, brother and sis—alone against the future was a perfect fit for young readers of the 1960s nuclear family.

Spiegle observed that *Space Family Robinson* "was a success right from the beginning, running about four years, for awhile one of their most popular. In fact, it was so popular that a television network stole our idea and refused to pay us any royalties. We were going to sue, but our lawyers cautioned against it, since we were doing so many comic books on their characters, and in the long run we would lose from loss of business to them. So we adopted their title and added it to ours in hope of deriving some publicity off the TV show."

The early 1960s marked the beginnings of a rapidly developing relationship between comic books and television science fiction shows. Initially drawing their inspiration from the comic books, the science fiction TV shows would eventually spawn their own comic book series.

TO BOLDLY GO WHERE NO COMIC BOOKS HAVE GONE BEFORE. . . .

"There is nothing wrong with your television set. Do not attempt to adjust the picture. We are controlling transmission. If we wish to make it louder, we will bring up the volume. If we wish to make it softer, we will tune it to a whisper. We will control the horizontal. We will control the vertical. We can change the focus to a soft blur or sharpen it to crystal clarity. For the next hour, sit quietly and we will control all that you see and hear. We repeat: There is nothing wrong with your television set. You are about to participate in a great adventure. You are about to experience he awe and mystery which reaches from the inner mind to . . . the OUTER LIMITS."

Outer Limits #5 © 1964 Daystar-Villa Di Stefano-United Artists

In the 1960s, television discovered science fiction and comic books discovered television. Never before or since would so many TV shows be based upon science fiction concepts and characters. At the same time, comic book publishers, which had long regarded TV as a competitor for their audience, began adapting dozens of popular television series for comic books.

Although there had been several juvenile science fiction television shows in the 1950s (*Captain Video, Buck Rogers, Space Patrol*, and *Tom Corbett, Space Cadet*) and a few more mature offerings (*Tales of Tomorrow, Out There,*

Science Fiction Theater), none had the impact of Rod Serling's *Twilight Zone,* which premiered on October 2, 1959.

For five years, nearly 18 million people on the average watched the *Twilight Zone* every week. In 1960, Dell Comics, which had already adapted such popular television shows as *I Love Lucy* and *Bonanza* for the comic books, obtained the rights to publish the *Twilight Zone* (March 1961) as a comic book.

Like the television series, the stories in the comic book also began with an introduction by Rod Serling:

"A strange light appears in the sky . . . one

among hundreds of *UFOs* . . . unidentified flying objects! The explanations for these sightings have been many and varied! The answer to this one can only be found in the *Twilight Zone!*"

The original *Twilight Zone* TV show lasted for 156 episodes, until 1964. The *Twilight Zone* comic book, however, outlasted the television show by another fourteen years. During its eighteen years of uninterrupted publication, the comic book featured nearly twice as many stories as appeared in the original television series.

Although none of the comic book stories was taken directly from the TV episodes, each usually had the Serling trademark of normal

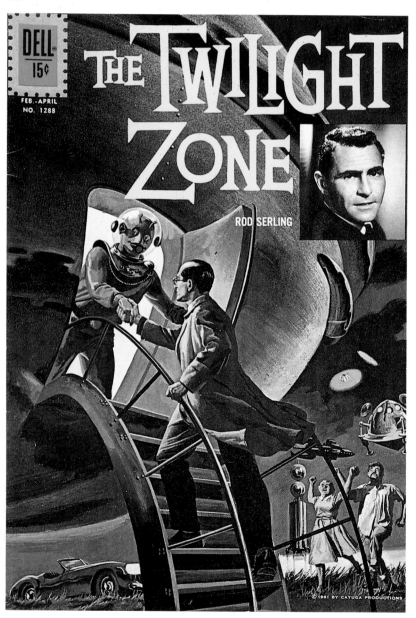

Twilight Zone #1288 © 1962 Cayuga Productions Inc.

people suddenly being plunged into weird situations: "Twelve o'clock noon. An ordinary scene, an ordinary city. Lunchtime for thousands of ordinary people. To most of them, this hour will be a rest, a pleasant break in the day's routine. To most, but not all. To Edward Hall, time is an enemy, and the hour to come is a matter of life and death."

After the *Twilight Zone*, the next major 1960s science fiction television series to arrive was ABC's *Outer Limits,* which premiered on September 16, 1963. Unlike the *Twilight Zone* mix of science fiction, fantasy, and horror, the *Outer Limits* took the springboard of hard science for its episodes about alien invaders, mutated freaks, and intergalactic visitors; in other words, the perfect visual material for comic books.

By the time the fourth episode ("The Man with the Power") was broadcast on October 7, 1963, viewers could also read the first issue of the *Outer Limits* comic book (January 1964). In order to appear so soon after the show's premiere, the early issues of the comic book had to be produced before either the writer or artist saw the *Outer Limits* on television. Nevertheless, comic book stories like "They Landed First" and "The Dread Discovery" fit right into the TV show's formula of having an alien bugaboo in every episode.

Along with *Outer Limits*, ABC was also broadcasting another science fiction program that year. Irwin Allen's *Voyage to the Bottom of the Sea*, set ten years in the future, followed the underwater exploits of Admiral Harriman Nelson and his atomic glass-nosed submarine, the Seaview. The popular series, which first aired on September 14, 1964, was inspired by Allen's 1961 movie of the same name. It was quickly adapted into a comic book by Gold Key (December 1964).

Another ABC science fiction series which was licensed by Gold Key as a comic book was *The Invaders* (October 1967). Roy Thinnes was the hero who witnesses an alien invasion but is unable to convince the authorities to believe his story. Although the same plot was used over and over, the paranoid fantasy was strong enough to last for 43 TV episodes and four comic book issues.

After his success with *Voyage to the Bottom of the Sea*, producer Irwin Allen next approached CBS with an idea for a "Swiss Family Robinson of outer space" television show. Premiering on September 15, 1965, the first episode of *Lost in Space* introduced us to the Robinson family, Dr. Zachary Smith, and the Robot ("That does not compute").

The TV show was so similar in concept to Gold Key's already existing *Space Family Robinson* comic book that the subtitle "Lost in Space" was added to the comic in 1965 to tie in with the show's popularity. In 1973, the book was officially renamed *Lost in Space*, although the comic never featured the evil Dr. Smith, the Robot, or any of the actual television characters.

Irwin Allen's next science fiction television series was *Time Tunnel*, which he produced for the 1966–67 season. The show about government time travelers proved interesting enough for Gold Key to adapt it as a comic book series (February 1967) on the chance that it might also turn into a hit like *Voyage to the Bottom of the Sea* or *Lost in Space*. Such was not the case and the show ended after one season with only two issues of the comic book published.

Another new 1966 science fiction television series, however, would fare much better on both the TV screen and the comic book pages.

"This is the Enterprise—a ship of the Star Fleet. Its five year mission in space: to probe the far reaches of the galaxy, to search the unknown and unlock its mysteries, to boldly go where no man has ever gone before!"

If that doesn't sound exactly like the introduction to the *Star Trek* television show, don't worry; it's actually from the first issue of Gold Key's *Star Trek* comic book (1967 July).

The early *Star Trek* comic books used photos from the TV show on their front covers and stills of the actors for inside cover features. Next to a picture of a bemused William Shatner in the first issue, Captain James Kirk is described as "a man of exceptional character and ability. He holds the loyalty and confidence of the entire crew. They would willingly follow him to the end of the universe. Before their mission is completed, they may have to."

The strong appeal of the *Star Trek* television show came from its characters: Captain

Star Trek #2 © 1968 Paramount Pictures Corp.

Kirk, Mr. Spock, Scotty, and Dr. McCoy. The early *Star Trek* comic books tried to capture some of the show's characterizations. When Captain Kirk returns aboard the Enterprise after having left Spock in charge, his first officer playfully tells him: "In fact, Jim, I enjoy being Captain so much, I may never turn back command to you! But," the logical Vulcan calmly adds as an asteroid hurtles toward the ship, "it's all academic if we don't get out of range fast!"

For the most part, however, the comic stories never had the opportunity to flesh out the men and women of the Enterprise. Sulu and Chekov were almost interchangeable,

Star Trek #7 © 1970 Paramount Pictures Corp.

Star Trek #33 © 1975
Paramount Pictures Corp.

fans turned to paperback novels and comic books for new stories about their favorite characters. Gold Key published the *Star Trek* comic book continuously until 1979 and also issued several collections of stories in the mid-1970s.

During the 1970s, other comic books continued to be adapted from popular science fiction television shows, such as *Space:1999* (November 1975), *Logan's Run* (January 1977), *Battlestar Galactica* (March 1979), and *Buck Rogers* (July 1979).

For all of their popularity, however, science fiction comics based on television shows are often unsatisfactorily derivative. Marty Pasko, who has written scripts for both the *Star Trek* comic book adaptation and the *Buck Rogers* television show, points out the obvious but critical difference between television film and comic books: "One moves, the other doesn't. And that makes a bigger difference than you might think. Comic books are essentially film in jump-cuts, film in which frames have been removed. There is a fluidity in film that you can't achieve in comics."

Mike Barr, another writer who has written for the *Star Trek* comic books, also agrees:

Scotty and Dr. McCoy were only in minor roles, and Lieutenant Uhura, one of the first black women in a continuing television series, was colored *white* in the comic books of the 1960s and early 1970s.

The first issue of the *Star Trek* comic book appeared in the summer of 1967 and the second issue came out almost a year later. The early *Star Trek* television show itself was far from a hit or popular series, having been threatened with cancellation several times. It would not be until the middle of 1969, with its fourth issue, after the *Star Trek* TV show was officially canceled, that the comic book would become a regular bimonthly series.

With the departure of *Star Trek* from TV,

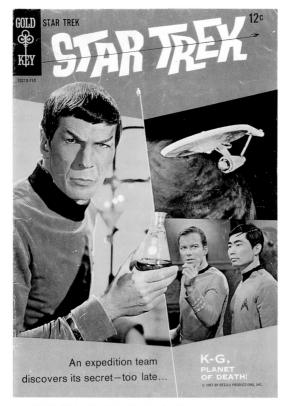

Star Trek #1 © 1967 Desilu Productions, Inc.

*Star Trek #33 © 1975
Paramount Pictures
Corp.*

"Comic books work better with the broad gesture, with things blowing up now and then. Which is not to say that you would not do a comic book *Star Trek* that is not the equal of the best TV *Star Trek* scripts, but some of the subtleties might be lost because the medium is static."

While Marv Wolfman, a comic book writer and former *Star Trek* editor, agrees that "you can never be as good as the TV show, because you don't have the actors saying the dialogue, even if you have better scripts, which is possible but not always likely. What we're trying to do, however, is take advantage of a medium that's published every month. We're doing stories that will build on each other, that

have continuity of characterization, that develop the Star Trek legend, stories that don't have to be wrapped up in the four acts."

Although there would have certainly been no *Star Trek* comic books without a *Star Trek* television show, perhaps there would have been no *Star Trek* without the early comic strips like *Buck Rogers* and *Flash Gordon* which made science fiction a popular visual medium. Regardless, the science fiction found in both comic books and on the television is cut from the same cloth.

The most striking use of science fiction comic book imagery, however, would not be found on television but on the bigger screen—at the movies.

BEAM ME UP, DARTH VADER

Science fiction comics and movies have enjoyed a give and take relationship ever since the 1936 *Flash Gordon* serial brought Alex Raymond's Sunday comic strip character to life on the screen.

Star Wars #1 © 1977 Twentieth Century-Fox Film Corp. Art by Howard Chaykin.

When science fiction movies became popular in the early 1950s, comic books adapted such films as *Destination Moon* and *Man from Planet X* and also provided the impetus for such movies as *Atom Man versus Superman* and *Superman and the Mole Men*. In the early 1960s, comic books like *Strange Tales* and *Amazing Adventures* borrowed heavily from earlier radioactive monster movies like *Them!* and the *Amazing Colossal Man*.

The happiest marriage of science fiction comic books and movies, however, occurred in the summer of 1977. George Lucas, a fan of comic books since the early 1950s, brought the ultimate science fiction pulp and comic book fantasy to life with the release of the first movie in his *Star Wars* trilogy.

Directed and written by Lucas, *Star Wars* was a visual smorgasbord of all the science fiction conventions and clichés which had been around since the days of Buck Rogers and Flash Gordon. Galactic empires, intelligent robots, a princess in peril, hot-rod spaceships, swashbuckling spacemen, and pop-eyed aliens were all taken from the likes of Saturday morning *Flash Gordon* serials and the pages of *Planet Comics*.

Lucas recalled that "I had decided I would make a film so rooted in the imagination that the grimness of everyday life would not fol-low the audience into the theater."

With its pyrotechnical visual effects and its action-fight-chase scenes, *Star Wars* was much closer to the science fiction found in comic books than in movies like *2001: A Space Odyssey* or *The Day the Earth Stood Still*. Lucas admitted that *Star Wars* was his attempt to bring back the high-adventure of "space opera" found in the 1930s *Flash Gordon* serials: "I'm trying to reconstruct a genre that's been lost and bring it to a new dimension so that the elements of space, fantasy, adventure, suspense, and fun all work together and feed off each other."

Dan Barry, who drew the *Flash Gordon* comic strip for nearly forty years, observed that *Star Wars* was in many respects like a comic book story: "It's written along more simplistic lines; it isn't science fiction at all, it's sheer fantasy, with no explanation of how things work or why, because that would slow down the story." Harry Harrison, who both wrote and drew science fiction comics in the 1950s, agreed that the "kind of modified science fiction that sells well in comics is action rather than ideas. And whatever ideas are there are usually physical basics. Zip, bang, boppo."

The zip, bang, and boppo of *Star Wars* made it an ideal candidate for the comic

Facing page: *Marvel Comics Super Special #16* © 1980 Lucasfilm, Ltd. Art by Al Williamson.

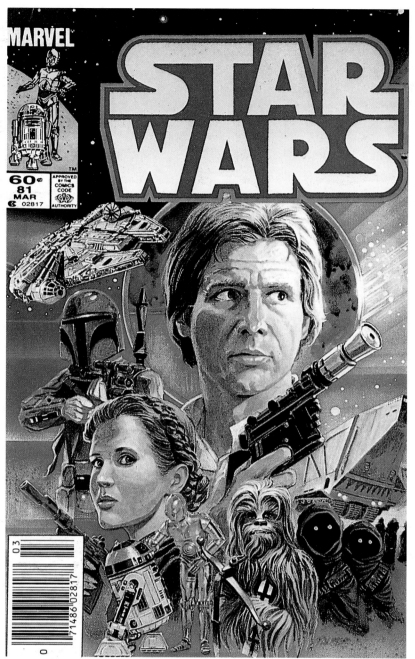

Star Wars #81 © 1984 Lucasfilm Ltd. Art by Tom Palmer.

counter with Hans Solo, Luke Skywalker, and Princess Leia was through the pages of a comic book.

With the movie adaptation under way, Thomas next met with Lucas and actor Mark Hamill (Luke Skywalker) to discuss the direction the comic book would take next. Since it would be three years before the sequel *The Empire Strikes Back* appeared, it was important that the monthly comic book not go off into any character or story development that would be contrary to the second movie.

The challenge that Thomas, and later Archie Goodwin and other *Star Wars* comic book writers, faced was this: how to keep the characters and their adventures interesting in an ongoing comic book series, but without any growth or development that might possibly contradict the second and the third *Star Wars* movies.

As a result, many *Star Wars* comic book stories are a look "behind the scenes" at the Alliance/Empire conflict, flashback adventures of the main characters, or the development of minor characters outside the movie mythos. The comic book was so successful that it ran for three more years after the release of the third movie, *Return of the Jedi*.

Mary Jo Duffy, one of the later writers on the *Star Wars* comic book series, recalled that after the third movie was released, "I was very

books and Lucas knew it. Even before filming began, the movie was licensed to Marvel Comics for adaptation.

Marvel writer and editor Roy Thomas remembered being shown "a dozen or so beautiful paintings of projected scenes from the movie . . . painstakingly detailed and breathtakingly beautiful. I was hooked."

Working from the shooting script and production sketches, Thomas and artist Howard Chaykin adapted the movie into six issues of a *Star Wars* comic book (July 1977). The first issue actually appeared several weeks before the movie was released. Our first en-

> "The first thing I look for is, while remaining true to comic book conventions, to adequately and enjoyably convey at least some of the experience of the movie . . . the biggest problem is trying to condense the material down."
>
> — *Archie Goodwin, adapter of* Alien, Blade Runner, *and* The Empire Strikes Back, *and other movies for comic books*

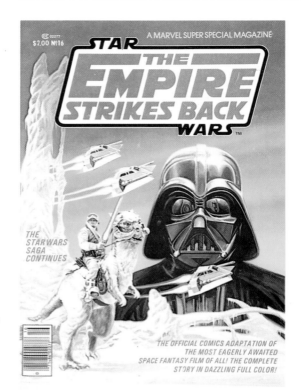

Marvel Comics Super Special #16 © 1980 Lucasfilm, Ltd. Art by Bob Larkin.

daunted by the notion that it was over." She did see, however, a creative opportunity to continue the series past the movies themselves. "Most of the characters survived and I see situations that are fraught with tension that lie ahead for them. During the entire time of the movies, all of the characters have had a set goal and cause in their mind and there is a very difficult problem to deal with and that is: what do you do when you have achieved your goals? How does each of them handle the problem of achieving their goals and how their reactions contrast? I am very interested in those people as characters. I think that the strength of it is that people care about those characters—they care passionately."

There was another set of science fiction characters that also aroused passionate care among their fans. At about the same time the *Star Wars* epic was unfolding, Captain Kirk, Mr. Spock, Scotty, and Dr. McCoy were all returning to the Starship Enterprise for *Star Trek—The Motion Picture* (1979).

The *Star Trek* movie, based on the popular 1960s television series, was another perfect property for comic books. The characters had

already proven their strong appeal with the comic book reading audience in their Gold Key comic series which lasted for 14 years— right up until the first *Star Trek* movie was released. With the appearance of the motion picture and the growing popularity of the *Star Wars* comic book and newspaper comic strip, it was only natural that the crew of the Enterprise return to the comic books.

The first three issues of the new *Star Trek* (April 1980) from Marvel Comics featured an adaptation of *Star Trek—The Motion Picture*. The comic book continued for nearly two years and was more faithful to the characters than the original Gold Key television comic

Star Trek #1 © 1980 Paramount Pictures Corp. Art by Steve Leialoha.

Marvel Comics Super Special #16 © 1980 Lucasfilm, Ltd. Art by Al Williamson From "The Empire Strikes Back."

book series. When the Enterprise crew encounters a race of alien gnomes, Scotty wisecracks to Captain Kirk: "Didna' they realize they'd come in contac' with th' Federation sooner or later? After all, tha's why we're in space—to go where *gnome* men have gone before?" Kirk groans and holds his head: "Ohh! Break us out of orbit, Mr. Sulu."

With the release of *Star Trek III* (1984), DC Comics obtained the rights to adapt the new movie and to also launch a third series of *Star Trek* (February 1984) comic books.

Tom Sutton, an artist who by his own admission had done "a lot of science fiction," was given the assignment of adapting *Star Trek III* (and later *Star Trek IV*). Sutton recalled

Star Trek #1 © 1989 Paramount Pictures Corporation. Art by Jerome Moore.

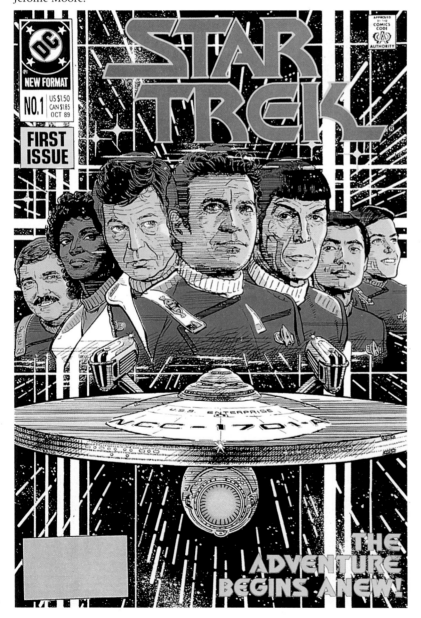

> "The interesting thing about the *Star Trek* TV stories is that, even in the dumb stories, there's the good character bits, interactions between Kirk, Spock, and McCoy, or the other characters. And that's something we hope to keep in the comic books. Because without the characters, you don't have *Star Trek*; you just have some guys in a spaceship that looks like the Enterprise."
>
> — *Mike Barr, writer,* Star Trek *(Marvel and DC Comics)*

that drawing the *Star Trek* adaptations was "a terrific amount of work because you go through all these stills and all these drawings and plans of the ships—it's not like doing a regular book where you more or less do it off the top of your head. Instead, they give you all these photographs, but you have to translate, to break these things down to comic book symbolism. Kirk can't have two chins, although he really does now, and Doc McCoy can't really be as weary as he really is, and Scotty's got to be a little more peppy than he was in the movie."

The comic book built upon the Star Trek mythos and also created new characters for the stories, like Bearclaw, Liz Sherwood, Konom, and Bernie the Klingon. The title, however, was suspended for a year before the next movie, *Star Trek V*, was released.

A new *Star Trek* series (October 1989) was reinitiated by DC Comics and was written by Peter David and drawn by James W. Fry. This time, however, editor Robert Greenberger recalled that the Star Trek movie people had asked them "to concentrate more on the original seven member cast and less on the

Marvel Comics Super Special #16 © 1980 Lucasfilm, Ltd. Art by Al Williamson.

original-to-comics cast." The new series jumped off from a tangential plotline in the *Star Trek IV* movie and culminated in the trial of James T. Kirk.

The *Star Wars* and *Star Trek* movies spawned two of the most successful science fiction comic book series ever. While the stories were occasionaly derivative and often limited by the constraints imposed by the movies, they introduced a new audience to science fiction comic books.

At the same time, however, science fiction comics seemed to be becoming subservient to the movies—another promotional spin-off to keep the characters and name in the public's eye. Perhaps it was time for the science fiction comic to look to the past and rediscover its heritage.

PAST PRESENT FUTURE PERFECT

Wise men—never mind which ones—have said that the last decade of a century often contains all the elements of the previous ninety-odd years. We try to take all of the past with us into that next hundred years, that next millennium, perhaps as a comfort blanket for the future. So a century rolls by in a decade, and in the last moments before the Future begins, the Past returns anew.

Flash Gordon #2 © 1988 King Features Syndicate, Inc. Art by Dan Jurgens.

That is true, at least, for science fiction comics.

As the 1990s began to age, nearly every major science fiction comic book title, character, or series of the previous decades made a return.

Buck Rogers, the father of all the science fiction comics, returned in a 1991 comic book series created by Flint Dille, the grandson of John Flint Dille, the original syndicator of the world's first science fiction comic strip in 1929.

In updating Buck for the 1990s, Dille wanted "to come up with a new take on the character that took us right back to the original intent of the strip during the 1920s and 1930s. There has always been a distinct look to Buck Rogers and his universe that we wanted to keep, but we wanted a scientific defensible look to the weaponry and the spaceships. What we're doing now is kind of the classical adventures in a plausible future. We decided to go with a hard science fiction, because with the advent of *Star Trek* and *Star Wars*, nobody was doing that anymore."

At the same time, Dille also realized that he was working with a cultural icon. "I've got dead ancestors looking over my shoulder," Dille remarked, "lurking around and watching to see what I'm going to do . . . we feel that there are things we can do and still keep Buck like the Buck everybody expects. The same will pretty much be the case with Wilma. Killer Kane will most likely remain totally treacherous and Ardala will always be a space slut."

The other popular comic strip spaceman of the 1930s, Flash Gordon, also got his chance for a respectful reprise more than fifty years after his debut. Written and drawn by Dan Jurgens, *Flash Gordon* (June 1988) kept the 1930s Art Deco design look of Alex Raymond but redefined the characters for a modern audience.

"There were a lot of things in the original Flash Gordon—the original Alex Raymond series—that we just could not do now," Jurgens recalled. "For example, Ming was an obvious result of the whole Yellow Peril with oriental paranoia overtones. We certainly

Facing page: *Vanguard Illustrated #3 © 1984 Cover art Al Williamson.*

Star Trek: The Next Generation #1 © 1989 Paramount Pictures Corp. Art by Jerome Moore.

couldn't keep it that way. When Raymond first did it, Ming was yellow. I decided to use the color gray, because one of the things I tried to do is make Mongo seem like a really decadent place—a place where you wouldn't want to be. The gray skin coloring helped in getting that across. It's dark and it's decadent."

The characters themselves, and especially the relationship between Flash and Dale Arden, also required some fine-tuning after fifty years. "There were many sexual overtones in the original," Jurgens observed. "Ming

wanted Dale and his daughter wanted Flash. It seemed as though every two or three weeks one or more of the women was in chains. Dale Arden was there to be brought along as a female so that she could be tied up on a rack or submitted to a whip. Dale didn't have a need to be a character then. I wanted a well-rounded character."

Some science fiction comics, however, seem in no need of updating. The EC science fiction comics, *Weird Science* and *Weird Fantasy*, have been reprinted over forty years after their first publication and still reach new readers.

Science fiction comics based on television programs of the 1950s and 1960s also found a new audience in the 1990s. *Tom Corbett, Space Cadet* (1991) came back to entertain the children of the parents who first watched the show on TV in 1950. *The Twilight Zone*, one of the longest-running science fiction comic books, returned in a 1990 series. Bill Mumy, who played young Will Robinson on the 1963 television series *Lost in Space*, became a consulting editor and writer in 1991 for a new comic book based on the characters and concepts in his original show.

Another 1960s science fiction series ripe for a 1990s revival was the man from AD 4000 —*Magnus, Robot Fighter*. Based on the character and designs created by Russ Manning in 1963, writer Jim Shooter and artist Art Nichols reinterpreted the popular robot-bashing comic book series for a new generation of readers.

Nichols wanted to to keep Manning's "really great futuristic world and his established designs of buildings, robots, and clothing intact as a foundation to go forward." Similarly, Shooter's intent was also to "honor the design and maintain the integrity of the future" as shown in the 1960s series, but also to let the characters gradually evolve for a 1990s audience.

"Look at Magnus' girlfriend, Leeja," Shooter remarked. "Issue after issue, she would ignore Magnus' instructions and warnings, get herself in trouble, and then cringe while he battled the robots, or be held hostage while he beat up the robots." Instead of immediately making her into a "macho, gun-toting mama," however, Shooter prefers to let "characters grow rather than making sweeping changes."

Another case of growing into the past was the appearance of the popular TV series *Star Trek: The Next Generation,* which immediately inspired a comic book series of the same name from DC Comics (February 1988). Closely based upon the characters and concepts in the new Star Trek TV series, the comic book provides a look at what goes on in between the television episodes. Interestingly, both sets of Star Trek characters—those from the original TV series of the past and those from the second TV series of the "future"—coexist in the present in two series of comic books.

Perhaps the title that best epitomizes the tendency of 1990s science fiction comic books to invent the future by rediscovering the past is Mark Schultz's *Xenozoic Tales* series.

The comic book is set in the future, after the Earth has undergone a massive geological upheaval which sent the human race underground for protection from the boiling lava

and noxious gases. "Four hundred and fifty years after it had sealed itself off, mankind returned to daylight, and was greeted by a radically altered world. . . . A world that logically should not exist. . . . A world populated by an unprecedented, eclectic ecosystem!"

Welcome to the Xenozoic Era, a time in the future where all the eras of the past, all the way back to the Paleozoic era of the great dinosaurs, now exist simultaneously in a world remade by volcanoes. Artist and writer Mark Schultz created a world where a guy and a beautiful babe in a 1950s hot-rod can challenge a brontosaurus to a drag race. In the Xenozoic Era, all the previous times in history have melded and produced a future that is at once familiar and yet mind-numbingly different.

Coupled with Schultz's art style, which is strongly reminiscent of 1950s science fiction EC artists like Williamson, Wood, and Frazetta, the stories in *Xenozoic Tales* are an effective homage to all the science fiction comic books of the past.

Like *Buck Rogers,* the first science fiction comic from 1929, the stories in *Xenozoic Tales* are also set in the 25th century. The more things change, the more they remain the same.

And perhaps therein lies the enduring popularity of science fiction comic books. After a Great Depression, after a World War (and several smaller ones), after atomic bombs and hydrogen bombs, after moon landings and Mars missions, science fiction comics have still prospered and remained with us.

As long as there is hope for the future, science fiction comics—or certainly their spirit—will be with us. Our perennial attempt at visualizing, predicting, and wrestling with tomorrow comes out in both cave paintings and comic strips. And in every case, there is that delight and that joy in the infinitude of human imagination that causes us to look, to read, and to wonder so deliciously about the future.

Xenozoic Tales #9 © 1988 Mark Schultz. Art by Mark Schultz.

Magnus Robot Fighter #1 © 1991 Voyager Communications, Inc. Art by Art Nichols.

SCIENCE FICTION COMICS

A Guide and Checklist

Science fiction has existed in the comic books since their very beginnings. If one includes the many superhero and fantasy-related titles, nearly half the comic books ever published would be science fiction under the broadest definition.

The following checklist is a guide to comic books which are primarily science fiction or outer-space related. For the most part, only comic books whose contents are almost exclusively science fiction are listed. Comic books containing superhero, horror, or mystery stories with only an occasional science fiction story are not included, unless the title is of special note.

For each title, the publisher is listed, as well as the dates and numbers of the first and last issues. Please note that not all titles start with issue #1. Comic books, especially those from the 1950s, sometimes changed publishers, content, and/or title and numbering might start in mid-series or suddenly begin over again. For example, the first issue of EC's *Weird Science* was #12 (May 1950) which is a continuation of the numbering from *Saddle Romances* #11, the title it replaced. The next three issues of *Weird Science* are #s 13, 14, 15, but with the fifth issue, the numbering begins with #5 and continues until it ends with #22. As a result, there are *two* different *Weird*

Science issue #s 12, 13, 14, 15.

For some titles, issue numbers are omitted from the beginning, end, or middle of a run because they did not contain science fiction stories. In other cases, issue numbers out of sequence simply reflect a certain publisher's esoteric numbering system.

In the description for each title, significant artists (when known) are listed, along with other information. The term "black and white" means that the comic was published in black and white instead of color. "Magazine" refers to comics published in a magazine-size format (about $1^1/2$" wider and longer than a comic book). "Reprints" indicate comics with previously printed science fiction stories.

Nearly all the major (and many minor) science fiction comic books published in the United States are listed as of publication time. Some titles, particularly low-circulation, black-and-white comics of the 1980s and 1990s, may have been overlooked due to limited distribution.

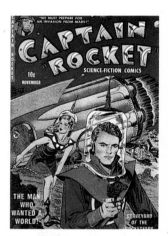

*Captain Rocket #1 ©
1951 Premier Publishing.
Art by Harry Harrison.*

Facing page: *Tales Calculated to Drive You Bats #3 © 1963 Close Up Publications*

Alien Encounters #7 © 1986 Cover Art Corey Wolfe.

Adventures on the Planet of the Apes
Marvel Comics
1975 October–1976 December
1–11

Based on characters and concepts from *Planet of the Apes* movie series. Reprints stories (in color) from *Planet of the Apes* magazine.

Alarming Adventures
Harvey Comics
1962 October–1963 February
1–3

Science fiction and suspense stories with art by Reed Crandall and Al Williamson (#1–3), Bob Powell (#2), and George Tuska (#1).

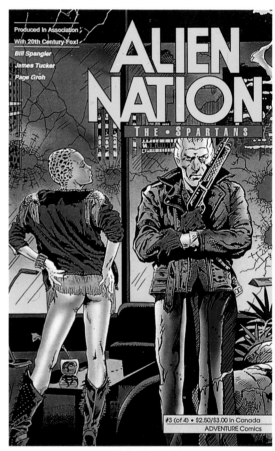

Alien Nation: The Spartans #3 © 1990 Twentieth Century-Fox Film Corp. Art by Paul Daly.

Adventures into the Unknown
American Comics Group
1955 March–1967 August
62–174

Considered one of the very first horror comics, the first 61 issues contain little science fiction. Later issues generally have at least one science fiction story with a superhero series (Nemesis) in #s 154–170. Art by Al Williamson (#s 91, 96, 107, 116, 128).

Alien Encounters

Eclipse Comics
1985 June–1987 August
1–14

An anthology title of extraterrestrial tête-à-tête with art by Tom Yeates, Steve Bissette, Rick Geary, John Bolton, and Richard Corben. Writers include Gardner Fox, Ray Faraday Nelson, and Len Wein.

Alien Fire

Kitchen Sink Press
1987
1–3

In the 21st century, diverse alien races have discovered Earth. They find our materialistic culture so quaint that a black market develops for 20th-century Earth artifacts—like Wurlitzer jukeboxes, Elvis Presley albums, and comic books. Written by Anthony Smith and drawn by Eric Vincent.

Alien Legion

Epic Comics/Marvel
1984 April–1990 August
Vol. 1 #1–20; Vol. 2 #1–18

The Alien Legion consists of interstellar warriors who fight for a common cause wherever they are needed. The second volume of the series continues two years after some Legionnaires have either been lost or killed.

Alien Nation

DC Comics
1988 December
1

Adaptation of 1988 movie about the integration of aliens into society.

Alien Nation: The Spartans

Adventure Comics
1990
1–4

Based on characters and concepts in television series based on the 1988 movie. Black and white.

Alien Worlds #5 © 1983
Cover Art John Bolton.

Alien Worlds

Pacific/Eclipse Comics
1982 December–1985 January
1–9; 3-D #1

Science fiction anthology with art by Al Williamson (#s 1, 4, 8), Dave Stevens (#s 2, 4), John Bolton (#5), and Roy Krenkel (#6). Richard Corben adapts a story by William F. Nowlan in #7. Scripts by Bruce Jones. Three-dimensional issue also published.

Aliens
Dark Horse
1988–1991
Vol. #1, 1–6; Vol. #2, 1–4; Vol. #3

Based on the characters and situations in the 1979 movie (*Alien*) and the following sequels. Volume #1 drawn by Mark A. Nelson; volume #2 drawn by Denis Beauvais. Mark Verheiden, the writer of the series, stated that he wanted to create a "cross between the total nightmarishness and creepiness of the first movie and the action of the second film. I think the strength of comic books can really gear toward both tenors." First appearance of series is in *Dark*

Aliens Vol 2 #4 © 1989 Twentieth Century-Fox Film Corp. Art by Denis Beauvais.

Aliens Vs. Predator #4 © 1990 Twentieth Century-Fox Film Corp. Art by Dave Dorman.

Horse Presents #24. Volume #1 in black and white; other issues in color.

Aliens: Earth Wars
Dark Horse
1990 June–1990 October
1–4

Based on concepts from 1986 movie *Aliens*. Covers by John Bolton.

Aliens, The
Gold Key
1967 September; 1982 May
1, 2

"For hundreds of years, Earthmen explored the stars, never once finding another inhabitant as intelligent as man!" Suddenly, in a star-cluster 3,000 light-years from Earth, contact is made with a race of aliens. After overcoming mutual suspicion and distrust, the Earthmen and aliens exchange crew members in order to learn more about each other. Originally a continuing series in *Magnus, Robot Fighter* (#s 1–28), the comic strip explored the difficulties alien races have in establishing peaceful contact. Drawn by Russ Manning, the comic reprints stories from *Magnus, Robot Fighter* #s 1, 3, 4, 6–10. The second issue (1982) reprints the first issue.

Aliens vs. Predator
Dark Horse
1990 June–1990 December
0–4

Based on characters and concepts in 1986 and 1989 movies. Issues #s 1–4 are in color; issue #0 reprints (in black and white) the prequel from *Dark Horse Presents* #s 34–36.

Amazing Adult Fantasy
Marvel Comics
1961 December–1962 July
7–14

Subtitled "The Magazine that Respects Your Intelligence," this fantasy comic specialized in short stories with surprise twist endings. Written by Stan Lee and drawn by Steve Ditko.

Amazing Adventures
Ziff-Davis Publications
1950 November–1952 Fall
1–6

When the publishers of *Amazing Stories,* the oldest science fiction magazine, decided to publish comic books, they hired Jerry Siegel, a longtime science fiction fan and Superman cocreator, as an editor and writer for this and other titles. Wally Wood turned in a 9-page story for the first issue and Murphy Anderson drew stories for #s 1–5.

Amazing Adventures
Marvel Comics
1961 June–1961 November
1–6

Each issue featured science fiction and fantasy stories drawn by Jack Kirby and

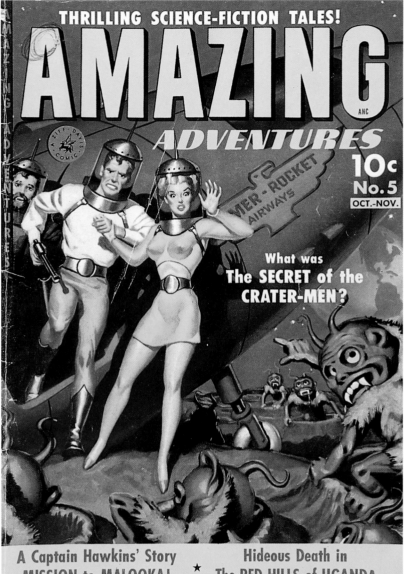

Amazing Adventures #5 © 1951 Ziff-Davis Publishing Company

Steve Ditko before the days of *Fantastic Four* and *Spider-Man.*

Amazing Adventures
Marvel Comics
1973 May–1976 November
18–39

It's AD 2018 and the Martians are in control of Earth. The surviving humans are either slaves or traitors who serve the Martian masters. Killraven, an Earthman trained as a gladiator for the sport of the Martians, becomes the leader of a rebel group. Editor Roy Thomas based the series upon the concepts in H. G. Wells' 1898 novel *War of the Worlds*. Thomas recalled that "the direct inspiration for the story was the chapter 'The Man on Putney Hill,' in which a visionary artilleryman talks at length about how life will be under the triumphant Martians." P. Craig Russell was the chief artist on the series (#s 28–32, 34, 37, 39) and Don McGregor wrote the majority of the stories.

Attack on Planet Mars © 1951 Avon Periodicals, Inc.

Astonishing
Marvel Comics
1951 October–1957 August
3–63 (no #1, 2)

Issue #s 3–5 feature science fiction stories and a hero named Marvel Boy. The remaining issues are a mix of horror, mystery, and science fiction stories. Artists included Reed Crandall, Bill Everett, Al Williamson, Bob Powell, Gene Colan, and Steve Ditko.

Attack on Planet Mars
Avon Comics
1951
1

Adaptation of Ray Cummings' 1930 novel *Tarrano the Conqueror*. Art by Joe Kubert, Wally Wood, and Carmine Infantino.

Basil Wolverton's Planet of Terror
Dark Horse
1987 October
1

Reprints Basil Woverton's science fiction-terror stories from *Journey Into Unknown Worlds* #7 (October 1941), *Marvel Tales* #102 (August 1951), *Mystic* #4 (September 1951), *Weird Tales of the Future* #3 (September 1952). Black and white.

Battlestar Galactica
Marvel Comics
1979 March–1981 January
1–23

Based on the characters and concepts in the 1978 television series and TV movie. Survivors of a doomed planet search for a new world while engaging in constant petty bickering. Issues #s 1–5 are direct adaptations of the TV movie. First three issues partially reprint *Marvel Comics Super Special* #8.

Beneath the Planet of the Apes
Gold Key
1970 December
30044–012

Adaptation of 1970 movie, the second in the *Planet of the Apes* series. Art by Alberto Giolitti. Contains pullout poster.

Black Hole
Western Publishing/Whitman
1980 March–1980 September
1 (11295)–4

First two issues adapt 1979 Walt Disney movie. Remaining issues based on characters and concepts. Art by Dan Spiegle.

Blade Runner
Marvel Comics
1982 October–1982 November
1–2

Adaptation of 1982 movie based on Philip K. Dick novel. Reprints *Marvel Comics Super Special* #22 with art by Al Williamson with Ralph Reese, Dan Green, and Carlos Garzon.

Blast-Off
Harvey Comics
1965 October
1

Contains stories originally created for the 1958 comic book *Race for the Moon* which were not used before the title was canceled. Stories by Jack Kirby and Al Williamson.

Blue Bolt
Star Publications
1950 August–1952 May
106–110, 113 (No S-F #s 111–112)

Basil Wolverton's Spacehawk stories from *Target Comics* (1941–42) are reprinted in #s 106–110, 113. Issue #113 (which was titled *Blue Bolt Weird Tales*) was reprinted as *Eerie Tales* #15 in 1964.

Brick Bradford
Standard/Better Publications
1948–49
5–8 (No #s 1–4)

Reprints book-length stories from the newspaper strips written by William Ritt and drawn by Clarence Gray. The comic book series coincided with the release of the 1948 *Brick Bradford* movie serial.

Buck Rogers
Eastern Color Printing Company/Famous Funnies
1940 Winter–1943 September
1–6

After a successful six-year run in *Famous Funnies*, Buck was awarded his own comic book in 1940. Issues #s 1–5 reprinted Sunday pages by Rick Yager. Issue #6 reprinted daily strips by Dick Calkins as well as an original 2-page story. The stories roughly parallel the Buck Rogers reprints in *Famous Funnies* #s 3–79.

Brick Bradford #6 © 1948 King Features Syndicate, Inc.

Blue Bolt #107 © 1950 Star Publications. Art by L.B. Cole.

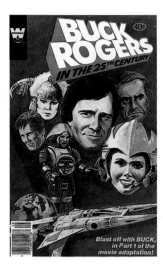

Buck Rogers #2 © 1979 Robert C. Dille

Buck Rogers
Gold Key
1964 October
1

Buck fights "The Space Slavers" in this original full-length comic book story.

Buck Rogers
Gold Key
1979 July–1982 May
2–9, 11–16 (No issue #10; see 1964 series for issue #1)

Based on the characters and concepts in the 1979–81 movie/TV series *Buck Rogers in the 25th Century*. The movie (which was a theatrical release of pilot for the television series) was adapted in #s 2–4.

Writers included Paul S. Newman and B. S. Watson. Artists included Frank Bolle (#s 2–4), Al McWilliams (#s 5–11), and Mike Roy.

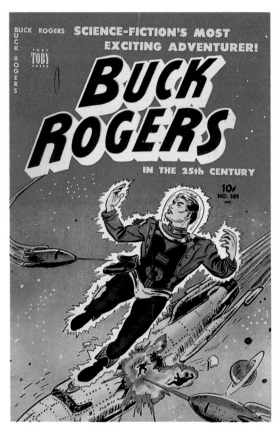

Buck Rogers in the 25th Century #101 © 1951 Toby Press

Buck Rogers
TSR, Inc.
1990
1–3

Revival of the first comic strip space-man. Each issue contains a game module and a tie-in with the Buck Rogers role-playing science fiction computer game.

Buck Rogers in the 25th Century
Toby Press
1951 January–1951 May
100, 101, 9

Reprints the "Modar of Saturn" adventure from the 1947–48 daily newspaper strips as drawn by Murphy Anderson. Robert Barton, a writer of adventure radio serials, scripted the story. The comic book also featured original stories. For example, in issue #101, Buck travels back to the 20th century to stop a communist revolution in Austria.

Captain Rocket
Premier Publishing
1951 November
1

Harry Harrison put this comic book together almost completely on his own ("I edited, wrote what I could, drew and inked it . . ."). Captain Rocket, otherwise known as Alan Campbell, "has dedicated his life to the development of super-scientific knowledge that would protect Earth from the *unknown forces* of the universe." Other series in the comic book include the Space Falcon, who "preys on the ill-gotten loot of crooked spacemen and donates it to the poor people of the universe," and Aurora of Jupiter, "a lovely scientist of the planet Jupiter who works for universal peace in her domed laboratory in the void of the stratosphere."

Captain Science
Youthful Magazines
1950 November–1951 December
1–7

Gordon Dane, aka Captain Science, is assisted by his sidekick Rip and girl-friend Luana in a secret laboratory in New Mexico. He receives instructions from an omniscient robot brain and has a fully gassed flying saucer at his immediate disposal. Wally Wood drew a story for #1. Issue #s 4, 5 have two stories each by Wood and Joe Orlando. Title changes to *Fantastic* with issue #8 and features a Captain Science story by Harry Harrison.

Captain Victory and the Galactic Rangers
Pacific Comics
1981 November–1984 January
1–13

Jack Kirby created, wrote, and drew the space adventures of Captain Victory, Major Klavus, Egg-Head, and the other Rangers who live by the slogan: "Victory is Sacrifice, but Sacrifice is Continuity!" Huh?

Captain Video
Fawcett Publications
1951 February–1951 December
1–6

Based on the 1949 television series and drawn by George Evans with assistance from Al Williamson. Evans recalled that "Al did mostly figures, for back then he wouldn't bother with what he didn't like to draw. It had to be fun as well as profitable! That was okay, though, for the mechanical gimmickry was stuff I could toss off the easiest."

Celestial Mechanics
Innovation Comics
1991
1–3

Widget Wilhelmina Jones is a freelance

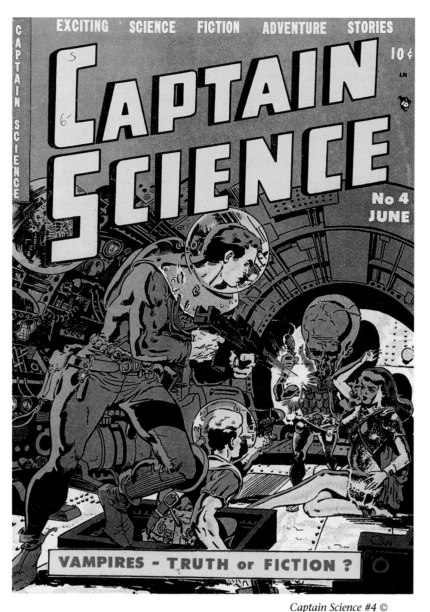

Captain Science #4 ©
1951 Youthful Magazines.
Art by Joe Orlando and
Wally Wood.

space mechanic trying to make an honest living in the 24th century. Black and white.

Classics Illustrated
Gilberton Publications
1947 February–1961 July
34, 47, 105, 124, 133, 138, 144, 149, 153, 160, 162, 163

Almost every major science fiction novel by H. G. Wells and Jules Verne was adapted for the *Classics Illustrated* line. Titles and artists are as follows: #34 (*Mysterious Island*, Robert Webb), #47 (*Twenty Thousand Leagues under the Sea,*

Classics Illustrated #124 © 1955 Gilberton Company, Inc. Art by Lou Cameron.

thing. Roy Krenkel developed the design of the rocket sphere itself. Williamson had fun with some of the non-human characters and the action shots. He made suggestions, as did Angelo Torres, who was by then deeply involved in what passed for science fiction in comic books."

Crusader From Mars
Ziff-Davis Publications
1952 January–1952 Fall
1, 2

Jerry Siegel wrote this series about an adulterous Martian couple (Tarka and Zira) who are banished to Earth in order to eliminate evil. Tarka and Zira's good deeds include destroying a bacteriological bomb and then spraying Midwestern grain fields with "radioactive phosphorous" to prevent a blight disease.

DC Science Fiction Graphic Novel
DC Comics
1985–87
1–7

Large format comic book with adaptations of works by Robert Bloch (#1), Ray Bradbury (#3), Harlan Ellison (#5), George R. R. Martin (#7), Larry Niven (#6), Frederik Pohl (#4), and Robert Silverberg (#2).

DC Super-Stars
DC Comics
1976 April–October 1977
2, 4, 6, 8, 16

Reprints 1950s and 1960s stories from these DC Comics science fiction series: "Adam Strange" (#s 2, 4, 6, 8), "Atomic Knights" (#2), "Space Ranger" (#s 4, 8), "Captain Comet" (#s 4, 6), "Tommy Tomorrow" (#6), "Space Cabby" (#6), "Star Rovers" (#8). "Star Hunters," a new series with art by Don Newton and Bob Layton, begins in #16.

H. C. Kiefer), #105 (*From Earth to Moon,* Alex A. Blum), #124 (*War of the Worlds,* Lou Cameron), #133 (*The Time Machine,* Lou Cameron), #138 (*Journey to the Center of the Earth,* Norman Nodel), #144 (*First Men in the Moon,* George Woodbridge and Al Williamson), #149 (*Off on a Comet,* Gerald McCann), #153 (*Invisible Man,* Norman Nodel), #160 (*Food of the Gods,* Tony Tallarico), #162 (*Robur the Conqueror,* Don Perlin), #163 (*Master of the World,* Gray Morrow). George Woodbridge, artist on *First Men in the Moon,* remembered that "everybody in the world worked on that

Doc Weird's Thrill Book
Pure Imagination Publishing
1987–88
1–3

Black-and-white reprints of early 1950s science fiction stories. Issue #1 reprints an Al Williamson and Frank Frazetta story from *Forbidden Worlds* #1. Issue #2 reprints a Wally Wood story from *Amazing Adventures* #1 as well as a Wood/Joe Orlando story from *Captain Science* #5. Issue #3 reprints a Joe Orlando/Wood story from *Captain Science* as well as a Wood story from *Space Detective* #1. All three issues serialize *Vic Torry and His Flying Saucer* by Bob Powell from 1950.

Doctor Who
Marvel Comics
1984 October–1986 August
1–23

Based on the British television show (1963) which reprints comic strips from

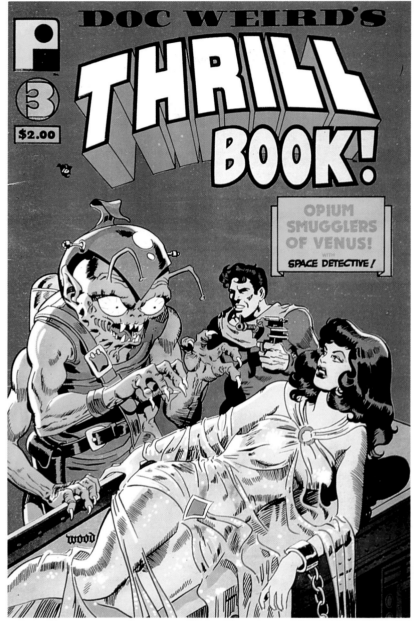

Doc Weird's Thrill Book #3 © 1988 Pure Imagination Publishing. Art by Wally Wood.

Doctor Who #7 © 1985 British Broadcasting Corp. Art by Dave Gibbons.

the UK *Dr. Who Weekly*. Dr. Who also appears in *Marvel Premiere* #s 57–60.

Dr. Who and the Daleks
Dell Publishing
1966 December
12-190-612

Adaptation of the 1965 movie which was inspired by the long-running British science fiction television series. Art by Dick Giordano and Sal Trapani.

Drift Marlo (Space Detective)
Dell Publishing
1962 May–1962 October
1(01-232-207)-2

Space-age investigator Drift Marlo keeps missile launch sites safe from enemy agents and saboteurs. Claire, his assistant and would-be girlfriend, is continually frustrated by his lack of personal interest in her ("Well, really! You . . . you . . . you *galaxy gumshoe!*"). Phil Evans wrote both the comic book and the newspaper comic strip which inspired it.

Earth Man on Venus © *1951 Avon Periodicals, Inc.* Art by Gene Fawcette.

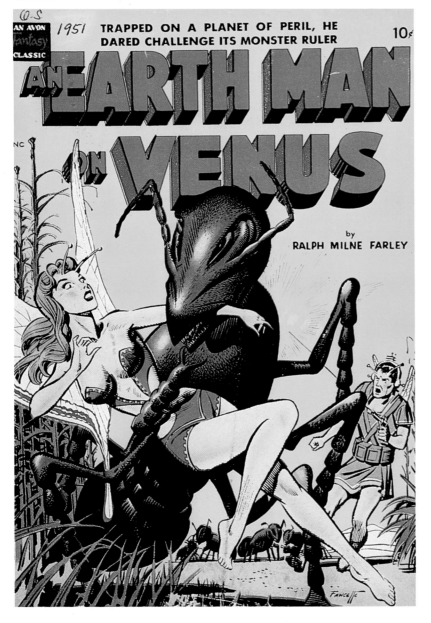

Dune
Marvel Comics
1985 April–1985 June
1–3

Adapts 1985 movie based on Frank Herbert's 1965 novel. Series reprints *Marvel Comics Super Special* #36.

E.C. Classic Reprints
East Coast Comix Company
1973 May–1976
1–12

Reprints EC comics in color. Science fiction issues include #2 (*Weird Science* #15, 1952), #5 (*Weird Fantasy* #13, 1952), #11 (*Weird Science* #12, 1950).

Earth Man on Venus
Avon Comics
1951
1

Comic book adaptation of a 1948 Avon paperback of the same name with artwork by Wally Wood (25-page story). Originally published as *The Radio Man* in 1924, the book by Ralph Milne Farley (pseudonymn of Roger Sherman Hoar) was the first in a series of Venusian adventures starring Myles Cabot. The comic book story was reprinted in *Strange Planets* #11.

Famous Funnies
Eastern Color Printing Company/Famous Funnies
1934 October–1955 July
3–190, 209–218 (Buck Rogers not in 1, 2, 191–208)

First science fiction series in a comic book. The Buck Rogers stories were reprinted from the Sunday comic strips by Rick Yager. Almost all were rewritten and relettered for the comic book. Issues 3–190 reprinted strips which appeared from 1933 to 1947 with only a few omissions. Later issues (209–218) did not reprint strips in order. Dick Calkins drew short stories for the comic book in issue #s 88, 94, 97. Another science fiction strip, *Speed Spaulding*, appears in #s 72–88. Drawn by Marvin Bradley, the 1940 comic strip was adapted from the 1933 novel *When Worlds Collide* by Edwin Balmer and Philip Wylie.

Fantastic Voyage
Gold Key
1967 February
10178-702
Adaptation of 1966 movie in which a medical team is shrunk to microscopic size so they can enter the body of a patient. Art by Wally Wood and Dan Adkins.

Fantastic Worlds
Standard/Better Publications
1952 September–1953 January
5–7 (no issues 1–4)
These three issues promised both "Amazing Planet *and* Space Adventures." Art by Alex Toth (#s 5, 6) and Murphy Anderson (#5).

Fantastic Worlds #7 © 1953 Literary Enterprises, Inc.

Drift Marlo #2 © 1962 General Features Corp.

Fawcett Movie Comic
Fawcett Publications
1950; 1952 February
(No Number), 15
Fawcett adapted several western, adventure, and science fiction movies for the comics. These two science fiction issues are *Destination Moon* (1950) with art by Curt Swan, and *Man from Planet X* (1952). *Destination Moon* was reprinted in *Space Adventures* #20 (March 1956) as "First Trip to the Moon" and again in *Space Adventures* #23 (May 1958). *Man from Planet X* was reprinted in 1987 under the same title.

Flash Gordon #3 © 1951
King Features Syndicate,
Inc.

First Men in the Moon
Gold Key
1965 March
10132-503

Adaptation of movie based on the 1901 novel by H. G. Wells. Drawn by Fred Fredericks, 1960s artist for the *Mandrake the Magician* newspaper comic strip.

Flash Gordon
Dell Publishing
1942–1953 November
10, 84, 173, 190, 204, 247, 424, 2, 512

Alex Raymond story sequences from the 1930s Sunday pages are reprinted in

#10 ("The Ice Kingdom") and #84 ("The Fiery Desert"). Later issues feature new stories written for the comic books with artwork by Paul Norris (#s 173, 190, 204, 246), John Lehti (#424), and Frank Thorne (#512, #2).

Flash Gordon
Harvey Comics
1950 October–1951 April
1–4

Each issue reprints approximately five months of Sunday strips by Alex Raymond from the late 1930s through 1941, along with 1–2 page filler features like "Stories behind the Stars" and "Know Your Planets." One such feature called "The World *You* Will Live In" told 1950s readers that someday "Telephone wires will line tomorrow's highways for two-way phone messages. When a driver wants to make a call, he lifts the receiver from the dashboard. The call is relayed to the requested party. If there is a call for the driver, his phone buzzer rings because the call's frequency will match his phone's frequency." Imagine that.

Flash Gordon
Gold Key
1965 June
1

Reprints *Flash Gordon* #173 (1947) with art by Paul Norris and a new cover.

Flash Gordon
King/Charlton/Gold Key/Whitman
1966 September–1982 March
1–37

The early issues by Al Williamson (#s 1, 4, 5) are generally considered some of the best drawn *Flash Gordon* comics outside of Alex Raymond's. Williamson recalled that "I really enjoyed doing those books more than just about anything else that I was doing. I love the whole idea of Flash so much, I think maybe it shows and the reader is attracted by that." Other artists include Gil Kane (#2), Ric Estrada (#3), Reed Crandall (#s 6, 8, 11, 12), Jeff Jones (#13), Mike Kaluta (#18), Mac Raboy (newspaper strip reprints, #7), and Alex Raymond (newspaper strip reprints, #s 9, 10). Issues #s 31–33 are serialized from the 1980 *Flash Gordon the Movie* comic book with art by Al Williamson.

Flash Gordon
DC Comics
1988 June–1989
1–9

Flash, Dale, and Ming get a 1980s makeover in this series written and drawn by Dan Jurgens.

Flying Saucers
Avon Comics
1950
1

Aliens wake up from a million-year nap inside a South American mountain and ferociously buzz the Earth in their con-

Flash Gordon #3 © 1967 King Features Syndicate, Inc. Art by Al Williamson.

veniently parked flying saucers. Their intentions, however, are ultimately friendly and they neutralize our atomic weapons so we won't blow our silly selves up. Wally Wood draws the 21-page story.

Flying Saucers #1 © 1967 Dell Publishing Co., Inc. Art by Frank Springer.

Flying Saucers
Dell Publishing
1967 April–1969 October
1–5

The stories were written as if based upon factual accounts, complete with made-up names, dates, and locations:

"On a warm July evening in 1966, Seaman Third Class Richard Grover, hitchhiking to his home in Vermont from the naval station in Groton, Connecticut, suddenly sees a sight that, if he lives through it, will never be forgotten!" Artists include Frank Springer, Sam Glanzman, and Sal Trapani.

Forbidden Worlds
American Comics Group
1955 August–1967 August
35–145

The first 34 issues (#s 1–34) are almost exclusively horror. Later issues generally have at least one science fiction story with a superhero series (Magicman) in #s 125–141. Art by Al Williamson (#s 63, 69, 76, 78) and Steve Ditko (#s 137, 138, 140).

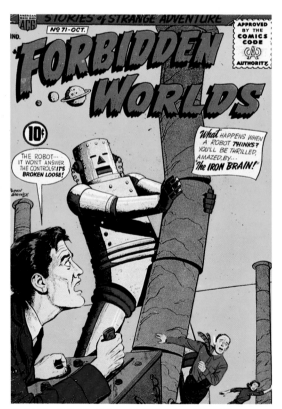

Forbidden Worlds #71 © 1958 Best Syndicated Features, Inc. Art by Ogden Whitney.

From Beyond the Unknown #6 © 1970 DC Comics, Inc.

From Beyond the Unknown
DC Comics
1969 October–1973 November
1–25

Reprints 1950s–1960s stories from *Strange Adventures* and *Mystery in Space* with art by Carmine Infantino, Murphy Anderson, Carmine Infantino, Sid Greene, and Gil Kane. Series reprinted include Space Cabby (#18), Space Museum (#s 23, 25), and Star Rovers (#s 18–22).

Funnies, The
Dell Publishing
1939 April–1941 June
30–56 (other issues not science fiction)

Edgar Rice Burroughs's *John Carter of Mars* was adapted for this comic book in a series drawn initially by Jim Gary and later by Burroughs's son, John Coleman Burroughs. The episodes were based on Burroughs's popular series of Martian novels, which began with *A Princess of Mars* (1912). In December 1941, John Burroughs turned the comic book series into a newspaper comic strip which lasted until 1943.

Future World Comix
Warren Publishing Company
1978 September
1

Magazine-size reprints of science fiction comics.

Galactic War Comix
Warren Publishing Company
1978 December
1

Magazine-size reprints of science fiction comics, with art by Wally Wood and Al Willliamson.

Green Planet
Charlton Comics
1962
1

Flying dinosaurs and blue-skin monkeys in an interplanetary adventure written by Joe Gill, Charlton Comics chief writer from 1955 to 1967.

Incredible Science Fiction
EC Comics
1955 July–1956 January
30–33

After the Comics Code took effect, Gaines changed the name of *Weird Science-Fantasy* to *Incredible Science Fiction,* since the word "weird" was damnably associated with the now-prohibited horror comics. Jack Davis, an artist usually remembered for his horror and war stories for EC, tried his hand at science fiction in issue #s 30, 32, 33. Bernie Krigstein drew a story for each issue. Artists rounding out the series included Wally Wood (#s 30, 31, 33), Joe Orlando (#s 30, 32, 33), and Al Williamson with Roy Krenkel (#s 31, 32). The last issue reprinted the antiracism story "Judgement Day" from *Weird Fantasy* #18.

The Invaders #1 © 1967
QM Productions

Invaders, The
Gold Key
1967 October–1968 October
1–4

Based on the characters and concepts in the 1967–68 ABC TV show. Only one man witnesses the advance invasion of Earth by aliens who can assume human form. When he tries to convince authorities that the aliens are slowly taking over society, nobody believes him. Art by Dan Spiegle.

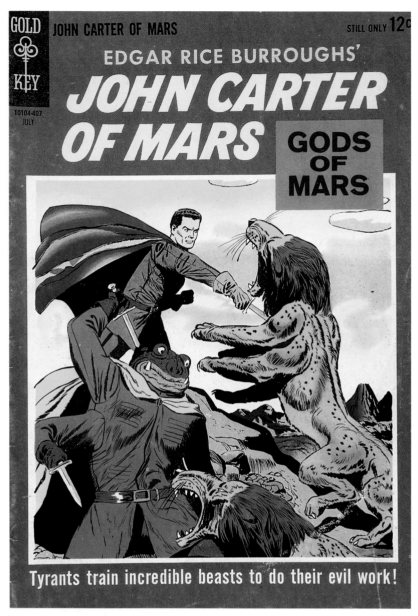

JOHN CARTER OF MARS — STILL ONLY 12¢

GOLD KEY

10104-407 JULY

EDGAR RICE BURROUGHS'

JOHN CARTER OF MARS

GODS OF MARS

Tyrants train incredible beasts to do their evil work!

John Carter of Mars #2 © 1964 Edgar Rice Burroughs, Inc. Art by Jesse Marsh.

Space Ace!" Both features were written by Gardner Fox. Bob Powell drew Jet Powers, while Al Williamson drew the Space Ace stories in # 3 (assisted by George Evans) and #4 (assisted by Wally Wood). Issues #s 1, 2 were reprinted in 1963 by IW Enterprises as *Jet Power* #1, 2.

John Carter of Mars
Dell Publishing
1952 January–1953 August
375, 437, 488

Adaptation of the first three Edgar Rice Burroughs Martian novels: *A Princess of Mars, Gods of Mars,* and *Warlord of Mars.* The comic book's characters and settings were faithful to the original books with art by longtime *Tarzan* comic artist Jesse Marsh and script by Phil Evans. All three issues were reprinted with new covers in 1964 by Gold Key.

John Carter, Warlord of Mars
Marvel Comics
1977 June–1979 October
1–28

Based upon the characters and concepts in Edgar Rice Burroughs's Martian novels. Instead of a strict adaptation of any one book, the stories in this series occur during an unaccounted-for nine-year gap by Burroughs in Chapter 27 of *A Princess of Mars.* Marvin Wolfman scripted the series. Art by Gil Kane in issue #s 1–10. Three annuals were also published (1977, 1978, 1979).

Jet Powers
Magazine Enterprises
1950–51
1–4

"This is Jet Powers! Captain of science, master of the atoms and molecules that make up the world we live in! Inventor and adventurer, his genius reflects itself in myriad ways, but always it is directed against the forces of evil that seek to wrest mankind from the paths of peace and plenty!" Also appearing with the modest Mr. Powers, as a secondary series, is that "star adventurer and pirate, law-bringer and fighter for justice—

Journey Into Mystery
Marvel Comics
1955 March–1962 July
23–82

Early issues are almost all horror/suspense stories with some science fiction beginning with issue #23. Art by Al Williamson (#s 33, 34, 43, 44, 54), Wally Wood (#39), Reed Crandall (#41), Jack Kirby (#s 51, 52, 56, 57, 60, 66, 69,

72, 76, 79, 80–82), and Steve Ditko (#s 33, 38, 50–82). With issue #83 (August 1962), the Mighty Thor begins, and science fiction stories disappear after issue #96.

Journey into Unknown Worlds

Marvel Comics
1950 September–1957 August
36–38, 4–59

The first issues (#s 36–38, 4–10) contain science fiction stories, while issue #s 11–33 are mostly horror. Later issues mix science fiction and horror/mystery. Stories by Basil Wolverton (#s 7, 14, 15), Reed Crandall (#s 48, 50, 53, 55, 59), Jack Davis (#s 44, 50), Al Williamson (#s 45, 55, 59), and Wally Wood (#51).

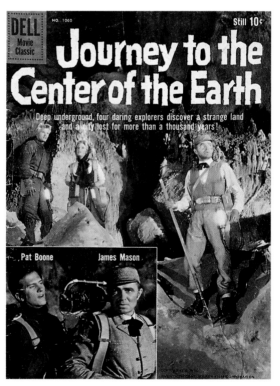

Journey to the Center of the Earth © 1959 Twentieth Century-Fox Film Corp.

Journey Into Mystery #71 © 1961 Marvel Entertainment Group, Inc. Art by Steve Ditko.

Journey to the Center of the Earth

Dell Publishing
1959 November
1060

Adaptation of 1959 movie starring James Mason and Pat Boone with art by John Ushler.

Kamandi, The Last Boy on Earth

DC Comics
1972 October–1978 September
1–59

"Earth has suffered a great disaster! When this happened is not known: the

Kamandi, The Last Boy on Earth #4 © 1973 DC Comics, Inc. Art by Jack Kirby.

must have been attractive to many readers, since this was the longest-lived of all the 1970s titles created by Kirby for DC Comics. (The origin from issue #1 is reprinted in #32.)

King Comics

David McKay Publications

1936 April–November 1949

1–145, 148–5 (issues 146, 147, 156–159, no science fiction)

The first newspaper strip reprints and comic book appearances of Flash Gordon and Brick Bradford. The *Flash Gordon* Sunday pages reprinted in issues 1–114 were drawn by Alex Raymond. After Raymond left the strip in 1944 to enter the Marine Corps, his assistant, Austin Briggs, took over and his art appears in later issues.

Land of the Giants #1 © 1968 Twentieth Century-Fox Film Corp.

records have been destroyed or buried beyond discovery! At any rate, no one seems to care except Kamandi, the last remaining human left on Earth! The rest of humanity has either changed or sunk to the level of beasts! As for the beasts—they've risen to the level once occupied by man! They walk and talk—and—make war once like man did! This is what Kamandi has stumbled into!" Written and drawn by Jack Kirby (#s 1–40), this series created a world that was a combination of *Tarzan*, *Planet of the Apes*, and *1,000,000 Years BC*. The fantasy of being the last teenager on Earth

Land of the Giants
Gold Key
1968 November–1969 September
1–5

Based on 1968–70 ABC TV show. Seven people in a "strato-cruiser" pass through a space warp and crash on a planet that is like 20th-century Earth, except that everything, including the planet's inhabitants, is 12 times larger.

Lars of Mars
Ziff-Davis Publications
1951 April–1951 July
10, 11

When Earth explodes its first H-Bomb, Martian scientists fear an atomic war. They send their hero, Lars, to Earth to ensure "interplanetary peace." He assumes a secret identity on Earth as an actor in a TV science fiction series and does plugs for Crackety-Wackety Cereal, the show's sponsor. The comic was created and written by editor Jerry Siegel, the cocreator of Superman. The series was drawn by Murphy Anderson, who recalled that "Jerry once handed me a story—a fifteen-page story—and he had written it on three legal-size pieces of paper, and it was all there—everything! All the dialogue and all the captions. But you see, he understood the medium so well, he didn't have to write out each panel." Stories from both issues were reprinted in three-dimensional comic format by Eclipse Comics in *Lars of Mars 3-D* (April 1987). The backup feature for Lars was "Captain Ken Brady, Rocket Pilot."

Last Starfighter
Marvel Comics
1984 October–1984 December
1–3

Adaptation of 1984 movie. Reprints *Marvel Comics Super Special* #31.

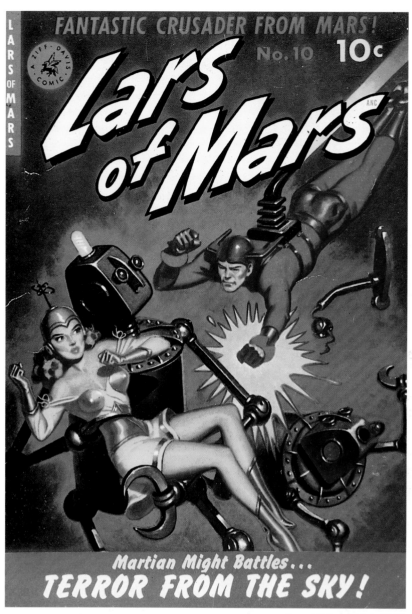

FANTASTIC CRUSADER FROM MARS!

A ZIFF·DAVIS COMIC

No. 10   10¢

Lars of Mars

Martian Might Battles...
TERROR FROM THE SKY!

Lars of Mars #10 © 1951 Approved Comics, Inc.

Logan's Run
Marvel Comics
1977 January–1977 July
1–7

Based on the 1976 movie and 1977 television show from the novel by William Nolan and George Clayton Johnson. People over the age of 30 must either commit suicide or be eliminated by sanctioned killers called the Sandmen. Art by George Perez (#s 1–5).

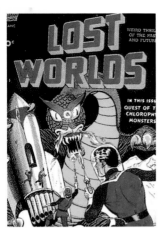

*Lost Worlds #5 © 1952
Visual Publications*

Lost in Space
Gold Key
1973 October–1982 May
37–59

Continuation of *Space Family Robinson* comic book with new title. Art by Dan Spiegle. Reprints in #s 49, 50, 55–59.

Lost in Space
Innovation Comics
1991
1–

Based upon the 1965 TV series, but set three years farther in the future. Writers include Bill Mumy and Mark Goddard, two of the actors from the original TV series.

Lost Planet
Eclipse Comics
1987 May–1988 February
1–6

Tyler Flynn makes an unexpected journey from Earth to the Lost Planet, a

Epidemic on Earth—and a fight for survival aboard the PLAGUE SHIP!

Lost in Space #59 © 1976 Western Publishing Company, Inc. Art by Dan Spiegle.

place where magic and mutants reign in a post-nuclear-ravaged world. Flynn's good buddies on the planet include a girlfriend named Romney and a chimp named Max. Written and illustrated by Bo Hampton.

Lost Worlds
Standard/Better Publications
1952 October–1952 December
5–6 (No 1–4)

Prehistoric worlds and outer-space monsters populate this comic book appropriately subtitled "Weird Thrills of the Past and the Future." Alex Toth's art appears in both issues.

Magnus, Robot Fighter
Gold Key
1963 February–1977 January
1–46

In the 41st century, mankind has become overly dependent upon robots. It's up to Magnus to karate-chop and destroy rogue robots which threaten the population. Art by Russ Manning (#s 1–21); later artists include Dan Spiegle, Mike Royer, and Paul Norris. Cover artist George Wilson. Writers include Don Christensen, Eric Freiwald, Kermit Shaefer, and Richard Kyle. Issues #s 22, 29–46 reprint the following issues: 1(#22), 2(#32), 6(#35), 7(#29), 8(#36), 11(#37), 12(#38), 13(#34), 14(#31), 15(#30), 16(#39), 17(#40), 18(#41), 19(#42), 20(#43), 21(#33), 23(#44), 24(#45), 25(#46). "The Aliens," a secondary series, appears in issue #s 1–28 with art by Manning (#s 1–21).

Magnus Robot Fighter
Valiant
1991 May–
0, 1–8+

The robot bashing continues in this updated version of the 1960s series. New stories written by Jim Shooter and drawn by Art Nichols. First eight issues

Magnus, Robot Fighter #17 © 1966 Western Publishing Company, Inc.

contain a cardboard insert of robot trading cards and coupons. Issue #0 is the prequel to the series.

Major Inapak the Space Ace
Magazine Enterprises
1951
1

Science fiction comics were reaching their height of popularity in 1951 when a breakfast drink manufacturer contracted with Magazine Enterprises to produce this "giveaway" comic book as an advertising premium for its customers. Drawn by Bob Powell, this spaceman from the future (1982!) was named after an instant chocolate milk drink mix that promised "clear skin, normal vision, good red blood, healthy appetite, and plenty of pep."

Man O'Mars
Fiction House
1953
1

Martians were big in the 1950s comics (*Lars of Mars, Crusader from Mars, John Carter of Mars*, etc.). This title featured the Space Rangers series from *Planet Comics* and art by Murphy Anderson. The comic was reprinted in 1964 by IW/Super under the same name.

Major Inapak the Space Ace © 1951 Magazine Enterprises. Art by Bob Powell.

Marvel Classic Comics

Marvel Comics

1976–78

2, 4, 11, 14, 21, 22, 25, 31

Jules Verne and H. G. Wells get the Marvel Classic comic book treatment in *Time Machine* (#2), *Twenty Thousand Leagues under the Sea* (#4), *Mysterious Island* (#11), *War of the Worlds* (#14), *Master of the World* (#21), *Food of the Gods* (#22), *Invisible Man* (#25), and *First Man in the Moon* (#31). Veteran writer Otto Binder adapted some of the books which were drawn by Gil Kane, John Buscema, Alex Nino, and others.

Marvel Comics Super Special #27 © 1983 Lucasfilm, Ltd. Art by Bill Sienkiewicz.

Marvel Comics Super Special

Marvel Comics

1977–85

3, 8, 15, 16, 22, 24, 27, 31, 33, 36, 37 (Science fiction)

Adaptations of various movies, including *Close Encounters of the Third Kind* (#3, art by Walt Simonson), *Battlestar Galactica* (#8), *Star Trek* (#15), *Empire Strikes Back* (#16, art by Al Williamson), *Blade Runner* (#22, art by Al Williamson), *Dark Crystal* (#24), *Return of the Jedi* (#27, art by Al Williamson), *The Last Starfighter* (#31), *Buckaroo Bonzai* (#33), *Dune* (#36), and *2010* (#37).

Marvel Presents

Marvel Comics

1975 December–1977 August

4–7, 9, 11, 12

In the year 3015, most of humankind is dead, conquered by the lizard–like Badoons. Among the survivors are the Guardians of Galaxy, a band of Earthlings and friendly aliens who seek to overthrow the Badoons. The Guardians consist of Major Vance Astro ("first Earthman to the stars, last survivor of the 20th century"), Charlie-27 ("last of Earth's Jupiter colony, genetically-engineered to withstand the enormous pressure and rampant radiation of the Jovian atmosphere"), Yondu ("last of the natives of Centauri-IV, site of Earth's only interstellar colony"), Martinex ("the last living member of Earth's colony on Pluto"), and the mysterious Starhawk (simply referred to as the "one who knows"). Art by Al Milgrom. First appearance in *Marvel Super-Heroes* #18. After an absence, the characters returned in their own comic book, *Guardians of Galaxy* (June 1990).

Marvel Special Edition

Marvel Comics

1977–78; 1980

1–3; 3; Vol. 2 #2

All extra-large-size (10" by 13") comics. Issue #1 reprints *Star Wars* #s 1–3; issue

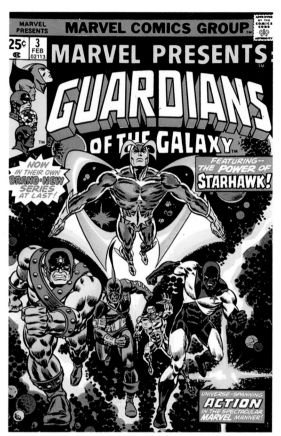

Marvel Presents #3 © 1976 Marvel Entertainment Group, Inc.

#2 reprints *Star Wars* #s 4–6; issue #3 (first) reprints *Star Wars* #s 1–6. Issue #3 (second) adapts *Close Encounters of Third Kind.* Vol. 2 #2 reprints adaptation of *The Empire Strikes Back* from *Marvel Comics Super Special* #16.

Mighty Samson
Gold Key
1964 June–1982 August
1–32

After the great nuclear war, mutated animals and savages rule the Earth. Mighty Samson is the eye-patched, animal-skin wearing hero. Art by Frank Thorne. Covers by Morris Gollub. Reprints in issue #s 21, 22, 32. The series "Tom Morrow" appears in issue #s 7–20. Tom, a mutant teenager with secret ESP powers, lives in Ultra City—"a thriving, bustling metropolis which has risen with civilization's rebirth after a nuclear holocaust."

Motion Picture Comics
Fawcett Publications
1952 May
110

This issue in Fawcett's series of movie adaptations featured *When Worlds Collide.* Veteran comic book writer Leo Dorfman turned the 1951 movie screenplay by Sidney Boehm into a 32-page script which was illustrated by George Evans. Al Williamson, who had worked with Evans since 1949, lent a hand on this issue and both artists drew themselves into the story.

Mighty Samson #9 © *1967 Western Publishing Company, Inc.*

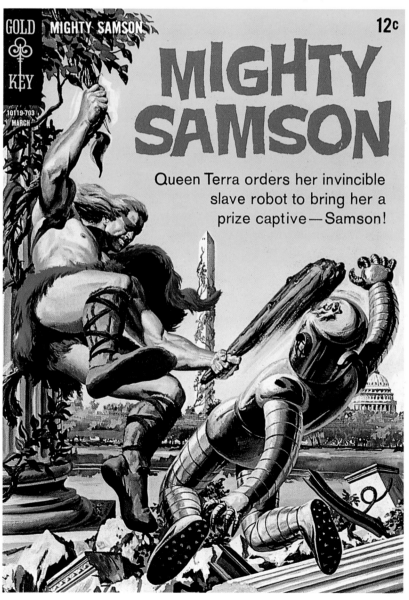

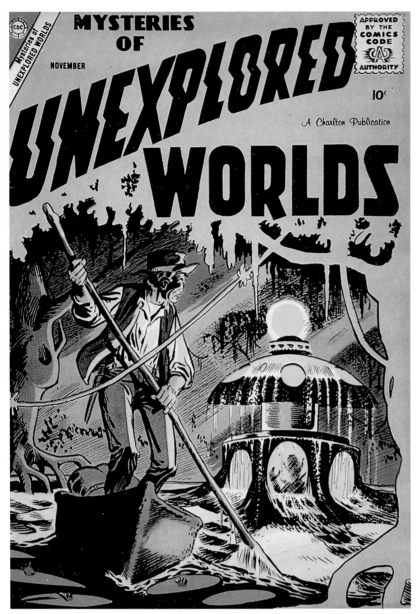

MYSTERIES OF UNEXPLORED WORLDS

Mysteries Of Unexplored Worlds #10 © 1958 Charlton Comics. Art by Steve Ditko.

Mysteries of Unexplored Worlds
Charlton Comics
1956 August–1965 September
1–48
A mix of science fiction and suspense with Steve Ditko art in issue #s 3–12, 19, 21–24, 26.

Mystery In Space
DC Comics
1951 April–1966 September
1–110 (1966); 111–117 (1980–81)
The second DC science fiction comic book. This title featured many artists and writers who worked on *Strange*
Adventures, also edited by Julius Schwartz. Art by Murphy Anderson (#s 2, 4, 8, 10, 12–17, 19, 45–48, 51, 57, 61–64, 70, 76, 87–98), Carmine Infantino(#s 1–8, 11, 14–25, 27–46, 48, 49, 51, 53–91, 103, 117), Gil Kane (#s 18, 100–102), and Steve Ditko (#s 111, 114–116). Regular series included "Knights of the Galaxy" (#s 1–8), "Interplanetary Insurance" (#s 16–25), "Space Cabby" (#s 21, 24, 26–47), "Adam Strange" (#s 53–100, 102), "Star Rovers" (#s 66, 69, 74, 77, 80, 83, 86), "Hawkman" (#s 87–90), and "Space Ranger" (#s 92–99, 101, 103).

Out of This World
Avon Comics
1950 June
1
Crom the Barbarian by John Giunta, plus two stories by Joe Kubert.

Out of This World
Charlton Comics
1956 August–1959 December
1–16
Science fiction and fantasy stories with art by Steve Ditko (#s 3–12, 16).

Outer Limits
Dell Publishing
1964 January–1969 October
1–18
Based on 1963–65 ABC television series. Early issues feature book-length stories. Issue #17 reprints #1; #18 reprints #2.

Outer Space
Charlton Comics
1958 May–1959 December; 1968
17–25; Vol. 2 #1
Science fiction tales from the beginning of the Space Race with art by Steve Ditko (#s 18–20, Vol. 2 #1).

Pirate (#s 12–65, 67–68, 70), Mars God of War (#s 15–35), Mysta of the Moon (#s 35–62, 68), The Lost World (#s 21–68, 70), Space Rangers (#26–37, 39–61, 63–64, 68, 70–71), Gale Allen and the Girl Squadron (#s 4–42, 65–66, 68–70), and Futura (#s 43–64). Issues #s 65–70 contain some reprints.

Artists include Matt Baker (Mysta), George Evans (Lost World), Graham Ingels (Lost World, Auro), Lee Elias (Space Rangers), Bob Lubbers (Space Rangers), Maurice Whitman (Star Pirate, Mysta), Murphy Anderson (Star Pirate), Nick Cardy (Lost World), Don Rico (Auro), Rudy Palais (Lost World),

Outer Space #20 © 1958 Charlton Comics

Phantom Planet #1234 © 1961 Four Crown Productions, Inc.

Outlanders

Dark Horse
1988 December–
1–25+

Japanese-style ("manga") science fiction stories. Black and white.

Phantom Planet

Dell Publishing
1961 December
1234

Adaptation of 1961 movie in which astronauts crash on a spaceship-asteroid inhabited by tiny aliens and a fast-moving monster. Art by John Lehti.

Planet Comics

Fiction House
1940 January–1953 Winter
1–73

The longest-running science fiction comic of the 1940s and early 1950s contained these major features: Auro, Lord of Jupiter (#s 1–7, 11–29, 41–61), The Red Comet (#s 1, 3–20,37), Star

*Planet Comics #1 cover
art © 1987 Dave Stevens.
Art by Dave Stevens.*

John Celardo (Red Comet), Fran Hopper (Mysta, Gale Allen), Lily Renee (Lost World), George Tuska (Space Rangers, Star Pirate), Bob Powell (Gale Allen), Rafael Astarita (Futura, Auro), and Leonard Starr (Star Pirate).

Planet Comics
IW/Super Comics
1964
1, 8, 9 (No other numbers)
> Reprints *Planet Comics* from 1953 (#1 reprints *Planet Comics* #70, #8 reprints #72, and #9 reprints #73). Also see *Space Mysteries* for reprint of *Planet Comics* #71.

Planet Comics
Blackthorne Publishing
1988
1–3
> New art and stories featuring Hunt Bowman from the 1940s *Planet Comics* series "The Lost World."

Planet of the Apes
Marvel Comics
1974 August–1977 February
1–29
> Based on characters and concepts from the movies *Planet of the Apes* (Issue #s 1–6), *Beneath the Planet of the Apes* (#s 7–11), *Escape from the Planet of the Apes* (#s 12–16), *Conquest of the Planet of the Apes* (#s 17–21), and *Battle for the Planet of the Apes* (#s 22–26). Black-and-white magazine.

Planet of the Vampires
Atlas Publishing
1975 February–1975 July
1–3
> Six astronauts return from a mission to Mars in 2010 only to find that Earth has been devastated by biological warfare. The remaining survivors are a band of savages and a super-scientific race of vampires. Welcome home!

Race for the Moon
Harvey Comics
1958 March–1958 November
1–3
> Editor Joe Simon put together this post-Sputnik comic book with artists Jack Kirby (penciler), Al Williamson (inker), Bob Powell, and Bill Draut. Writers included Ed Herron and brothers Dick and Dave Wood.

Rex Dexter of Mars
Fox Features Syndicate
1940 Fall
1
> After a successful introduction in *Mys-*

tery Men Comics (August 1939), Rex became the first science fiction character created for the comic books to have his own title. Dick Briefer drew this issue as well as most of Rex's appearances in *Mystery Men Comics*.

Robotman of the Lost Planet

Avon Comics
1952
1

Giant robots squash the human race and rule the Earth until a band of survivors send them packing. Art by Everett Raymond Kintsler.

Rocket Comics

Hillman Periodicals
1940 March–1940 May
1–3

"Rocket" Riley is the star of all three issues but he graciously shares his comic with super-guys like the Phantom Ranger, Buzzard Barnes, and Red Roberts the Electro Man.

Robotman of the Lost Planet #1 © 1952 Avon Periodicals, Inc.

Rocket Kelly

Fox Features Syndicate
1944; 1945 Fall–1946 October
1–5

Professor Kelly of the Mt. Glacier Observatory builds "weapons of war to help the governments maintain the peace of the world." One of his inventions is a shiny red, tri-fin rocketship which he gives to his son, appropriately nicknamed Rocket. Rocket, with his girlfriend Sue and sidekick Punchy, use the rocketship to fight Earthly crime and thwart interplanetary invasions. Sue was mostly window dressing for Rocket's rocket, while Punchy provided questionable comic relief: "Keep your eyes on the controls, applehead! We're entering a field of orbitless planetoids. One collision with them and you'll be apple sauce!" Rocket Kelly first appeared in the back pages of *Green Mask* #10 (August 1944). He also buzzed about in several other 1940s comics, including *Bouncer* #11–14 (September 1944–Spring 1945), *All Great* (1945), *Everybody's Comics* (1944), and *Book of All Comics* (1945).

Rocket Ship X

Fox Features Syndicate
1951 September
1

Given the track record of Victor Fox, the exploitive publisher behind this book, it's a safe assumption that he published this comic book in an attempt to cash in on a 1950 movie called *Rocketship XM*.

Rocket to the Moon

Avon Comics
1951
1

Adaptation of Otis A. Kline's 1930 novel *Maza of the Moon*. Art by Joe Orlando with assistance by Wally Wood.

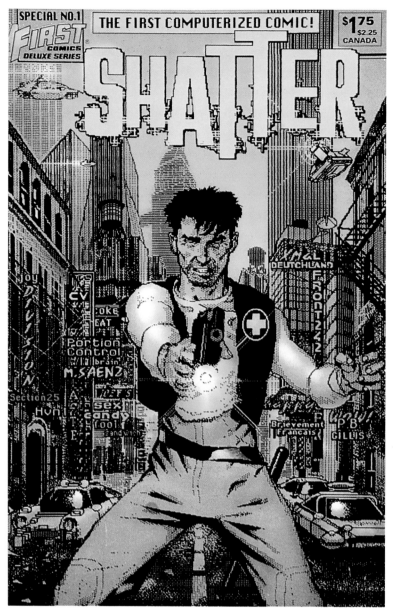

Shatter #1 © 1985 First Comics, Inc. Art by Micael Saenz.

Rocketman
Farrell Publications
1952 June
1

The comic book reprises the 1940s Rocketman superhero. Cal Martin first appears as the Rocketman in *Scoop Comics* (November 1941), when he invents a rocket backpack (nearly three years before the Republic Pictures Saturday morning serial *King of the Rocketmen*). Together with his girlfriend Doris (Rocketgirl) and his sidekick Billy (Rocketboy), Rocketman also jetted

about in *Punch Comics* (July 1944), *Major Victory Comics* (1945), and *Red Seal Comics* (1947).

Shatter
First Publishing
1985 June; 1985 December–1988 April
1; 1–14

Jack Scratch, a 21st-century private eye, has a series of dark and gritty adventures in *Shatter,* the first computer-generated comic book, with artwork by Michael Saenz.

Space: 1999
Charlton Comics
1975 November–1976 November
1–7

In 1999, men and women from all over the world staff an early-warning defense base on the moon. When a thermonuclear explosion knocks the moon out of orbit and sends it careening through the universe, the residents of Moonbase Alpha look for another planet to inhabit. Adaptation of 1975 television show, with art by Joe Staton (#s 1, 2) and John Byrne (#s 3–6).

Space: 1999
Charlton Comics
1975 November–1976 November
1–8

Based on 1975 television show, with art by Gray Morrow (#s 1–3, 5–8). Black-and-white magazine with articles and photos on TV show.

Space Ace
Magazine Enterprises
1952
5

The Space Ace was created by the veteran team of writer Gardner Fox and artist Fred Guardineer. Both men had worked together in comics and on science fiction series since the 1930s. The character originally appeared in the first seven issues of *Manhunt* (October 1947) and also in *Jet Powers* (1950).

Space Action
Ace Magazines
1952 June–1952 October
1–3

Stories of space-hardened men and women in "unusual interplanetary adventures." In "Beware the Human Meteorites," our hero Cosmo and his girlfriend Napthaili take on a bunch of kamikaze (living!) meteorites that bomb planets. "Suddenly, as Cosmo's spaceship was half-way between moon and Earth, several of the human meteorites, guided by Deuel's controlling rays, traveling with their usual frightening speed and unexpectedness, struck the ship and tore it apart! The force of the explosion blew Cosmo and Napthaili into airspace, while the meteorite monsters swept on their destructive way. . ."

Space Adventures #3 © 1952 Charlton Comics. Art by Dick Giordano.

Space: 1999 #3 © 1976 ATV Licensing, Ltd. Art by John Byrne.

Space Adventures
Charlton Comics
1952 July–1979 March
1–60 (no #22); Second series 2–8 (no
   #1); Third series (9–13)
   The first half-dozen issues feature "Rex Clive and the Space Officers" and art by Dick Giordano. Later issues (#s 15–18) feature Rocky Jones, Space Ranger, which was based on a juvenile TV show. Issue #s 20, 23 reprint the 1950 comic book adaptation of the movie *Destination Moon*. Steve Ditko's Captain Atom superhero series appears in #s 33–40, 42, with other Ditko stories in #s 10, 11, 24–27, 31, 32. Ditko art is also in the second *Space Adventure* series (1968–69, #s 2, 5, 6, 8), as well as in the third series (1978–79), which reprints the Captain Atom stories.

Space Busters

Ziff-Davis Publications
1952 Spring–1952 Fall
1–3

Earth is invaded from outer space and it's up to Brett Crockett and the Space Busters to stop them. Battles with Martian dwarfs and brass-bosomed Amazons in stories drawn by Bernie Krigstein (#s 1–3) and Murphy Anderson (#2). Covers by Norman Saunders.

Space Busters #1 © 1952 Approved Comics, Inc. Art by Norman Saunders.

Space Detective

Avon Comics
1951 July–1952 July
1–4

Rod Hathway, Space Detective, investigates such cases as the "Metal Murders of Mars," "Batwomen of Mercury," "Mole Women of Jupiter," and "Sea Nymphs of Neptune." Wally Wood designed and drew the character for the first issue.

Space Detective

IW/Super Comics
1964
1, 8, 9

Issue #1 reprints *Space Detective* #2 (1951); #8 reprints "Barney Carr, Space Detective" from *Famous Funnies* #191.

Space Family Robinson

Gold Key
1962 December–1969 October
1–36

Craig and June Robinson, and their children Tim and Tam, are the first family to live in their very own space station. Mom, Dad, and the kids not only peacefully coexist in such confined quarters, but even cooperatively conquer and defeat the occasional pesky alien invader. Art by Dan Spiegle. Cover art by George Wilson. Written by Del Connell, Gaylord DuBois, and others. Title changes to *Lost in Space* with issue #37.

Space Funnies

Archival Photography
1990
1

Reprints Spacehawk stories by Basil Wolverton from *Target Comics* #s 5–7 (June–August 1940).

Space Family Robinson #2 © 1963 Western Publishing Company, Inc. Art by George Wilson.

Space Man

Dell Publishing

1962 January–1964 March; 1972

1253, 1–10

On May 6, 1961, an Atlas rocket carried Commander Alan Shepard into a 15-minute suborbital space flight. A few months later, Dell Comics created this series about astronaut heroes of the future. Issue #9 reprints #1253; #10 reprints #2.

Space Mysteries

IW/Super Comics

1964

1, 9

Issue #1 reprints *Journey Into Unknown Worlds* #4 (April 1951); #9 reprints *Planet Comics* #71 from 1953.

Space Patrol

Ziff-Davis Publications

1952 Summer–1952 November

1, 2

Based on the 1950 ABC radio and

1951–52 television shows, with script by Phil Evans. Bernie Krigstein did some of the interior art and Norman Saunders painted both covers.

Space Squadron

Marvel Comics

1951 June–1952 February

1–5

Captain Jet Dixon has assembled a space squadron of "fighting rocket-men" to help him in the year 2000. Fighting with Captain Dixon are Blast Revere ("The Universe Is His Backyard"), Dawn Revere ("She Lives with

Space Man #6 © 1963 Dell Publishing Co., Inc.

Spacehawk #1 © 1989 Dark Horse Comics, Inc. Art by Basil Wolverton.

Death at Her Side"), Rusty Blake ("A Boy Today, Guardian of the Stars Tomorrow"), and Mxxptrm ("Mighty Warrior of Mars").

Space Thrillers
Avon Comics
1954
1

A 25-cent comic book consisting of three rebound comics—usually *Robotmen of the Lost Planet,* an issue of *Strange Worlds,* and another Avon comic book.

Space War
Charlton Comics
1959 October–1964 March
1–27 (1959–64); 28–34 (1978–79)

As the Space Race and Cold War between the U.S. and the USSR heated up in the late 1950s, this comic book played upon our fears with stories about outer-space bombardments and alien guided missiles. Steve Ditko stories in #s 4–6, 8, 10, 28–31, 33, 34. Issue #s 28–34 are mostly reprints.

Space Western
Charlton Comics
1952 October–1953 August
40–45

Previously published as *Cowboy Western Comics,* the comic was changed into a hybrid science fiction title with the early 1950s boom in space comics. Although early issues had some straight western tales, the comic book was mostly about Spurs Jackson and his Space Vigilantes. As science fiction comic sales declined in 1953, the title was changed back to *Cowboy Western Comics* with issue #46 (which, incidentally, featured one last space-western story).

Spacehawk
Dark Horse
1989–90
1–3

Each issue contains two "Spacehawk" stories by Basil Wolverton reprinted from *Target Comics,* as well as a new story drawn by other artists. Black and white.

Space Mysteries #1 © 1964 I.W. Enterprises

Spaceman, Speed Carter

Marvel Comics

1953 September–1954 July

1–6

Speed Carter and his "Space Sentinels" performed in stories drawn by Joe Maneely and George Tuska (#5).

Spanner's Galaxy

DC Comics

1984 December–1985 May

1–6

Polaris Spanner is an intergalactic fugitive with the handy powers of teleportation. Art by Tom Mandrake.

Star Hunters

DC Comics

1977 October–1978 October

1–7

Series begins in *DC Super-Stars* #16 (October 1977) with art by Don Newton and Bob Layton.

Star Trek

Gold Key

1967 July–1979 March

1–61

Based on the 1966–68 television series. Issue #s 1–9 have covers with photographs from TV show. Artists include Nevio Zaccara, Alberto Giolitti, Al Mc-Williams, and Mike Roy. Writers include Dick Wood, Allan Moniz, Len Wein, Arnold Drake, John Warner, Gerry Boudreau, Paul S. Newman, and George Kashdan.

Star Trek

Marvel Comics

1980 April–1982 February

1–18

Based on the 1979 movie *Star Trek: The Motion Picture*. Artists include Dave Cockrum, Gil Kane, Mike Nasser, Klaus Janson, Luke McDonnell, and John Buscema. Writers include Marv Wolf-

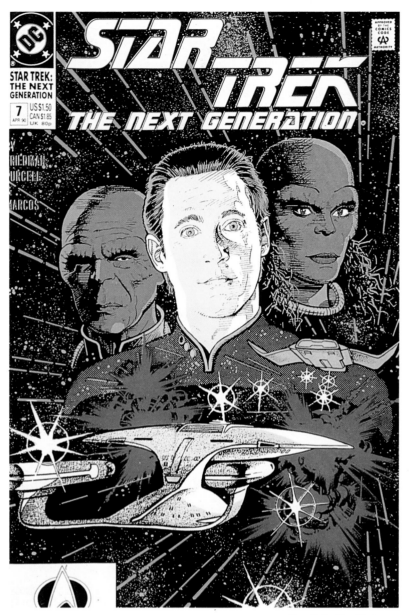

man, Marty Pasko, and Mike Barr. Issue #s 1–3 reprint the *Marvel Comics Super Special* (#15) adaptation of movie.

Star Trek: The Next Generation #7 © 1990 Paramount Pictures Corp. Art by Jerome Moore.

Star Trek

DC Comics

1984 February–1988 November

1–56

Based on *Star Trek* characters and movie series. Writers include Mike Barr, Diane Duane, Bob Rozarkis, Robert Greenberger, Mike Carlin, Tony Isabella, and Peter David. Artists include Tom Sutton (#s 1–6, 8–18, 20–27, 29, 31–34, 39–52,

Star Trek #16 © 1981 Paramount Pictures Corp. Art by Luke McDonnell.

55), Gray Morrow (#s 28, 35, 36, 56), Dan Spiegle (#19), and Dave Cockrum. Issue #33 celebrated the 20th anniversary of the TV show. A *Star Trek* Annual was also published in 1985, 1986, 1988.

Star Trek
DC Comics
1989 October–
1–10+

Based on characters and concepts from the *Star Trek* movie series. Written by Peter David and drawn by James W. Fry.

Star Trek Movie Special
DC Comics
1984 June, 1987, 1989
1, 2, 1

Based on *Star Trek* movie series. Issue #1 (1984) adapts *Star Trek III*, #2 adapts *Star Trek IV*, both with art by Tom Sutton; #1 (1989) adapts *Star Trek V*.

Star Trek #47 © 1987 Paramount Pictures Corporation Art by Tom Sutton.

Star Wars: Return of the Jedi #1 © 1983 Lucasfilm, Ltd. Art by Al Williamson.

Star Trek: The Next Generation
DC Comics
1986 February–1988 July
1–6

Based on the characters and concepts in television show. Six-issue limited series written by Mike Carlin and drawn by Pablo Marcos.

Star Trek: The Next Generation
DC Comics
1989 October–
1–12+

Based on the characters and concepts in television show. Written by Michael Jan Friedman and drawn by Pablo Marcos.

Star Wars
Marvel Comics
1977 July–1986 September
1–107

Based on the *Star Wars* movie trilogy.

First six issues adapt the 1977 *Star Wars* movie; issue #s 7–38 are based on characters and concepts in first movie. Issue #s 39–44 serialize the adaptation of *The Empire Strikes Back* movie (previously published in *Marvel Super Special* #16). Issue #s 45–79 based on characters and concepts in second movie. Issue #s 80–107 based upon characters and concepts in third movie. Three annuals published (1979, 1982, 1983). Artists include Howard Chaykin (#s 1–10), Carmine Infantino (#s 11–15, 17–37), Al Williamson (#s 39–44, 50, 98), Mike Golden (#38), Walt Simonson (#s 16, 49, 51–63, 65, 66). Writers include Roy Thomas, Archie Goodwin, and Mary Jo Duffy.

Star Wars in 3-D
Blackthorne Publishing
1986–88
30, 47, 48
Adventure on the ice planet Hoth from *The Empire Strikes Back*. Printed in "three-dimensional" format. Written by Len Wein.

Star Wars: Return of the Jedi
Marvel Comics
1983 October–1984 January
1–4
Adaptation of 1983 movie, third in series. Art by Al Williamson.

Starslayer
Pacific Comics/First Comics
1981 September–1985 November
1–34
Described as a "Robert E. Howard in outer space" hero by writer John Ostrander, Starslayer is a displaced Gaelic warrior who chops, hacks, and plunders his way across the universe. Issue #2 features the first appearance and origin of the Rocketeer by Dave Stevens. Artists include Mike Grell, (#s 1–7), Tim Truman, and Tom Sutton (#s 17, 20–22, 24–27, 29–33).

Steve Zodiac and the Fireball XL-5 #1 © 1963 Independent Television Corp.

Starstream
Western Publishing Company/Whitman
1976
1–4
Adaptations of classic science fiction stories. Issue #1 (John Campbell, Chad Oliver, Howard Goldsmith, Barrington J. Bayley, Joan Hunter Holly, Raymond Banks), #2 (Dean Koontz, Larry Niven, Robert Silverberg, Mary Schaub), #3 (Jack Williamson, Theodore Sturgeon, A. E. van Vogt, Anne McCaffrey), #4 (Paul Anderson, Isaac Asimov, Stephan Goldin, Robert Bloch). Each issue is 64 pages long. Most stories reprinted in

Strange Adventures #150
© 1963 DC Comics, Inc.
Art by Murphy
Anderson.

the 1977, 224-page comic *Questar Illustrated Science Fiction Classics*.

Steve Zodiac and the Fireball XL-5

Gold Key

1964 January

1

Steve Zodiac flies his spaceship, the XL-5, with a loyal crew of three: Professor Matthew Matic, Robert the Robot, and the blonde, lisping Dr. Venus ("Steve, as your space doctor, I insist zat you have more of ze food pills and zis coffee . . . "). Steve and his crew are headquar-

tered in Space City and receive their fighting instructions from Commander Zero (a name to inspire confidence). The comic was based on the Saturday morning children's televison show by Gerry Anderson which used puppets instead of live actors, similar to Anderson's other show, *Supercar*.

Strange Adventures

DC Comics

1950 August–1973 October

1–244

DC Comics's premier science fiction comic book. Regular series include: Chris KL-99 (#s 1–3, 5, 7, 9, 11, 15), Darwin Jones (#s 1, 66, 70, 79, 84, 88, 93, 149, 160), Captain Comet (#s 9–44, 46, 49), Space Museum (#s 104, 106, 109, 112, 115, 118, 121, 124, 127, 130, 133, 136, 139, 142, 145, 148, 151, 154, 137, 161), Star Hawkins (#s 114, 116, 119, 122, 125, 128, 131, 134, 137, 140, 143, 146, 149, 152, 155, 158, 162, 173, 176, 179, 182, 185), Atomic Knights (#s 117, 120, 123, 126, 129, 132, 135, 138, 141, 144, 147, 150, 153, 156, 160; reprints #s 217–231), Star Rovers (#s 159, 163; reprints #s 232, 233, 234, 236), Space Cabby (reprint #219), and Adam Strange (#222; reprints #s 217–221,223–244). Superhero series included Animal Man (#s 180, 184, 190, 195, 201) and Deadman (#s 205–216). Art by Murphy Anderson (#s 8–52, 94, 96, 97, 99, 115, 117, 119–163), Virgil Finlay (#s 2, 3, 6, 7), Carmine Infantino (#s 10–101, 106–151, 154, 157–163, 180, 190), and Gil Kane (#s 8–116, 124, 125, 130, 138, 146–157, 173–186). Reprints begin #217.

Strange Galaxy

Eerie Publications

1971 February–1971 August

Vol. 1, #8–#11

Combination of horror and science fiction stories, some new and some reprints. Typical stories are ballyhooed as follows: "Hole In The Sky—Panic

Strange Galaxy Vol. 1 #11 © 1971 Eerie Publications, Inc.

gripped a city when a monster dropped through a hole in the sky . . . Terror Asteroid—Paralyzing and blood-chilling horror on a bleak asteroid between Earth and Mars . . . Vampires From Dimension X—The winged monsters poured from a dimension in time like squealing rats hungry for blood!" Black-and-white magazine.

Strange Planets
IW/Super Comics
1964
1, 8, 9–12, 15–18
Reprints of 1950s science fiction comics with new covers. Issue #1 reprints *Incredible Science-Fiction* #30 (1955); #9 reprints *Strange Worlds* #4 (1951); #10 reprints *Space Detective* #1 (1951); #11 reprints *Earthman on Venus* (1951); #12 reprints *Rocket to the Moon* #1 (1951); #15 reprints *Journey Into Unknown Worlds* #8 (1951); #16 reprints *Strange Worlds* #6 (1951); #18 reprints "Space Busters" story (1952).

Strange Tales
Marvel Comics
1955 April–1962 September
35–100
Early issues are almost all horror/suspense stories with some science fiction stories after #34. Art by Steve Ditko (#s 46, 50, 67–100), Joe Orlando (#s 41, 44, 46, 49, 52), Jack Kirby (#s 67–100), and Reed Crandall (#s 53, 56, 66). With issue #101, the Human Torch becomes the lead feature, and science fiction stories disappear after issue #113.

Strange Worlds
Avon Comics
1950 November–1955 September
1–9, 18–19 (No 10–17)
An early science fiction comic with several continuing series. Gardner Fox wrote many of the stories, including "Crom the Barbarian" and "Kenton of the Star Patrol." Artists include Wally Wood (#s 2–5), Joe Orlando (#s 3–5), Al Williamson, Frank Frazetta, and Roy Krenkel (#3). Issue #18 reprints *Attack*

Strange Tales #94 © 1962 Marvel Entertainment Group, Inc. Art by Jack Kirby.

on *Planet Mars*; #19 reprints *Robotmen of the Lost Planet*. Issue #9 reprinted as *Strange Worlds* #5 by IW/Super (1964).

Strange Worlds
Marvel Comics
1958 December–1959 August
1–5

When Jack Kirby began drawing for Marvel Comics in 1958, this was the first new title that featured his art (issue #s 1,3). Steve Ditko, who had also just begun his association with Marvel, drew a story for every issue of this pre-

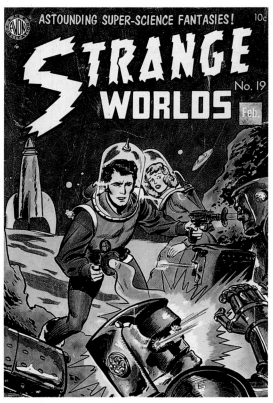

Strange Worlds #19 © 1955 Avon Periodicals.

dominantly science fiction title. Al Williamson art in #s 2, 4. The first issue is devoted to flying saucers.

Super DC Giant
DC Comics
1976 Summer
27

This all-science-fiction issue was subtitled "Strange Flying Saucer Adventures." Reprints 1950s–60s stories by Gil Kane, Russ Heath, Sid Greene, and others.

Superworld Comics
Komos Publishing
1940 April–1940 August
1–3

Hugo Gernsback, the publisher of the first science fiction magazine, noticed in late 1939 (before the first issue of *Planet Comics* appeared) that there was no comic book devoted exclusively to science fiction. Gernsback commissioned Frank R. Paul, his original artist

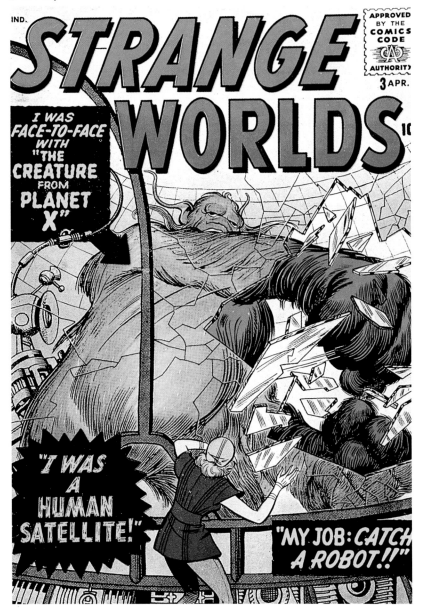

Strange Worlds #3 © 1959 Marvel Entertainment Group, Inc. Art by Jack Kirby.

for *Amazing Stories,* to draw the artwork for his new publication, *Superworld Comics.* He also enlisted the aid of Charles D. Hornig, one of his former editors of *Wonder Stories,* to write one of the comic's features, Buzz Allen, Invisible Avenger. Other regular features included Hip Knox, Super Hypnotist, and Mitey Powers, an interplanetary troubleshooter. Gernsback was so confident he had a winner, he scheduled issues 4 and 5 for publication. Poor sales, however, prompted him to leave the comic book business after only three issues.

Tales of Suspense
Marvel Comics
1959 January–1963 February
1–38

A blend of monster and fantasy stories by Jack Kirby, Steve Ditko, and Don Heck. Also, art by Al Williamson (#1, 4), Reed Crandall (#12). Issue #39 introduces Iron Man, and science fiction stories disappear completely after issue #48.

Tales of the Unexpected #16 © 1957 DC Comics, Inc.

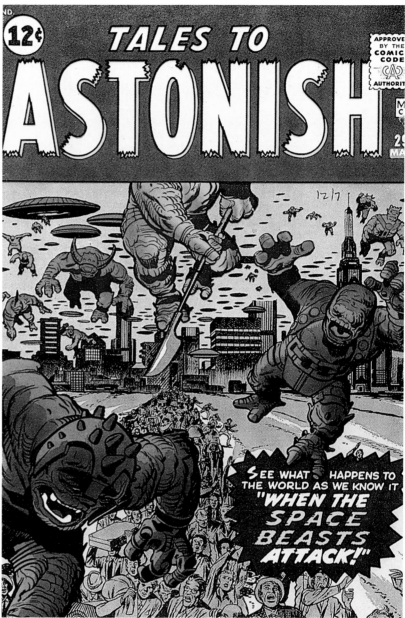

Tales To Astonish #29 © 1962 Marvel Entertainment Group, Inc. Art by Jack Kirby.

Tales of the Unexpected
DC Comics
1956 February–1967 December
1–104

The third DC science fiction title of the 1950s. Like *Mystery In Space* and *Strange Adventures,* the comic often featured science fiction stories with twist endings. Editor Jack Schiff, however, generally used different artists and writers than those who worked on the two DC science fiction titles edited by Julius Schwartz. Early issues feature art by Jack Kirby (#s 12, 13, 15–18, 21–24), Bill Ely,

Howard Purcell, John Prentice, and Mort Meskin. Later issues feature the Space Ranger (#s 40–82) as drawn by Jim Mooney, Bob Brown, and Phil Kelsey.

Tales to Astonish
Marvel Comics
1959 January–1962 August
1–34

A mix of monster, fantasy, and science fiction stories with art by Jack Kirby and Steve Ditko in nearly every issue. Other artists include Al Williamson (#5) and Jack Davis (#1). Issue #35 begins the Ant-Man/Giant-Man superhero series, although occasional science fiction stories still appear until issue #44.

The 3-D Zone
Renegade Press/Ray Zone
1987–89
1–26

Comic books adapted for "three–dimensional" effect. Science fiction issues

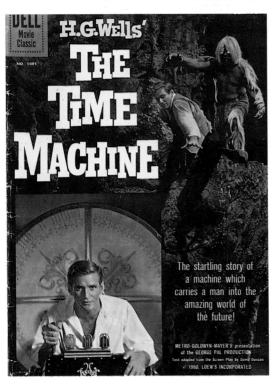

The Time Machine #1085 © 1960 Loew's Incorporated.

Thrilling Science Tales #2 © 1990 Americomics. Art by Mark Heike.

in the series include #13 (*Flash Gordon*—Sunday pages reprinted from 1936 serial, "Water World of Mongo"), #16 (*Space Vixens*—Dave Stevens cover and art), and #18 (*Spacehawk*—Basil Wolverton reprints).

The Time Machine
Dell Publishing
1960 March
#1085

Adaptation of 1960 movie produced by George Pal, based on the 1895 H. G. Wells novel. Art by Alex Toth.

Thrilling Science Tales
AC Comics
1989–90
1, 2

Reprints 1950s science fiction stories (some in black and white) with original stories as well. Issue #1 reprints a Space Ace story by Fred Guardineer, as well as stories by Frank Frazetta, Wally Wood,

Joe Orlando, and Al Williamson. Issue #2 reprints a Captain Science story by Wally Wood and a Captain Video story by George Evans.

Time Bandits
Marvel Comics
1982 February
1

Adaptation of 1981 movie which explores the ruptures of the time/space continuum with tongue firmly in cheek.

Time Tunnel
Gold Key
1967 February–1967 July
1, 2

Based on 1966–67 television series about two men trapped in a government time-travel experiment.

Time Warp
DC Comics
1979 October–1980 June
1–5

Science fiction anthology (64 pages) with art by Steve Ditko (#s 1–4), Joe Orlando (#2), and Gil Kane (#2).

Tom Corbett, Space Cadet
Dell Publishing
1952 January–1954 September
378, 400, 421, 4–11

Adaptation of 1950–52 television series, with art by Al McWilliams (#s 378, 400, 421), John Lehti, and Frank Thorne.

Tom Corbett, Space Cadet
Prize Publications
1955 May–1955 September
Vol. 2 #1–Vol. 2 #3

Prize Publications picked up the comic book rights to Tom Corbett after Dell Comics left the series. Mort Meskin drew some of these stories.

Tom Corbett, Space Cadet Vol 2 #2 © 1955 Videofeatures Company. Art by Mort Meskin.

Tom Corbett, Space Cadet
Eternity Comics
1990 January–1990 April
1–4

Based on characters and concepts in 1950–52 television show. Black and white.

Trekker
Dark Horse
1987 May–1989
1–9

Mercy St. Clair is a trekker—a bounty hunter of the future—who hunts her

GOLD KEY

TWILIGHT ZONE   ROD SERLING   12¢

THE TWILIGHT ZONE

10016-602
FEBRUARY

One lone defender battles insurmountable odds to halt the invaders from outer space!

*Twilight Zone #14 © 1966
Cayuga Productions Inc.*

men and aliens with cool professionalism and smoldering sensuality. Issue #7 features origin. Written and illustrated by Ron Randall. Black and white.

Twilight Zone
Dell/Gold Key/Whitman
1961 March–1982 May
1173, 1288, 01-860-207, 12-860-210, 1–92
Comic book adaptation of 1959–64 television series. Artists include Reed Crandall (#s 1173, 1288, 01–860–207, 1, 13–15, 21, 25, 26, 43), George Evans (#s 1173, 1288, 01–860–207, 1, 25–27, 32), Al Williamson (#s 12, 14, 51), Joe Orlando (#s 19, 20, 22, 23), Al McWil-

liams, Frank Boyle, and Mike Roy. Covers by George Wilson.

Twilight Zone
Now Comics
1990 November–
1–6+
Based on television series. Art by Neal Adams (#1).

2001: A Space Odyssey
Marvel Comics
1976 December–1977 September
1–10
Jack Kirby took the concepts from Stanley Kubrick's 1968 movie and Arthur C. Clarke's novel and fashioned his own mythology and vision of the future for this series. Kirby said that he built upon the movie's idea of "an alien power shaping the course of our evolution, doing so for purposes beyond our understanding, injecting ingredients we're not aware of, and changing a natural order to one of its own design." Kirby populated the title with his own cast of cosmically bizarre characters (Vira the She-Demon, Marak the Merciless, etc.) and mercilessly throttled the storyline between past, present, and future.

2001: A Space Odyssey
Marvel Comics
1976 October
1
Large size (84 pages, 10" by 13") adaptation of Stanley Kubrick's 1968 movie, with script and art by Jack Kirby. Throughout the comic book, Kirby uses astronomical photographs of the moon and planets as part of his page design and artwork.

2010
Marvel Comics
1985 April–1985 May
1, 2
Adaptation of 1984 movie sequel to

2001: A Space Odyssey. Reprints *Marvel Comics Super Special #37.*

UFO and Alien Comix
Warren Publishing Company
1978 January
1

   Stories by Alex Toth, John Severin, and others. Black-and-white magazine reprints.

UFO and Outer Space
Gold Key
1978 June–1980 February
14–25

   Continuation of *UFO Flying Saucers* title with reprints from that title in issue #s 14–16, 24, 25.

UFO Flying Saucers
Gold Key
1968 October–1977 January
1–13

   Stories about true and nearly true en-

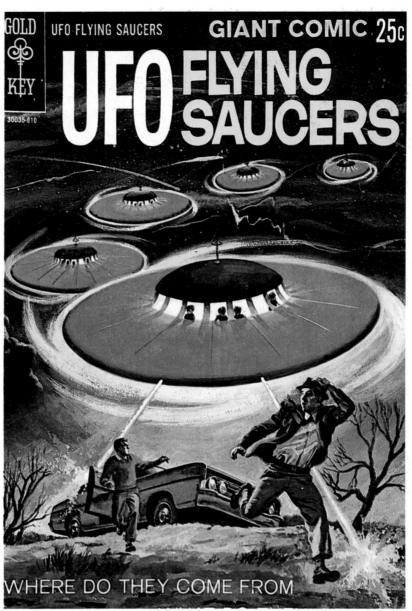

UFO FLYING SAUCERS

GIANT COMIC 25¢

UFO FLYING SAUCERS

WHERE DO THEY COME FROM

UFO Flying Saucers #1 © 1968 Western Publishing Company, Inc.

counters with unidentified flying objects. First issue is 68 pages long; rest are 36 pages. Art by Frank Bolle (#s 4–13). Stories reprinted in 1978 in both *UFO Encounters* #1192 (228 pages), #114004 (128 pages), and *UFO Mysteries* #11400, #11404 (96 pages).

Uncanny Tales
Marvel Comics
1952 June–1957 September
1–56

   The first 28 issues contain 2 to 3 science fiction stories. Art by Reed Crandall (#9), Joe Orlando (#s 49, 50, 53), and Al Williamson (#51).

#1 IN A TWO ISSUE LIMITED SERIES

2010

2010 #1 © 1985 MGM/UA Entertainment Corp. Art by Tom Palmer.

Unknown Worlds

American Comics Group
1960 August–1967 August
Code Approved 1–57

Science fiction and supernatural stories shared equal billing in this offspring of *Forbidden Worlds* and *Adventures Into The Unknown*. Art by Steve Ditko (#s 49, 50), Johnny Craig (#s 36, 47), and Al Williamson (#47–reprint).

Unknown Worlds of Science Fiction

Marvel Comics
1975 January–1975 November
1–6, Annual

Adaptations of stories by science fiction

Unknown Worlds of Science Fiction #1 © 1975 Marvel Entertainment Group, Inc. Art by Kelly Freas.

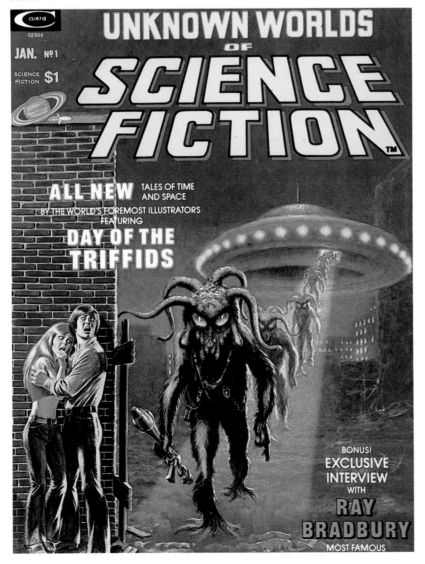

Unknown Worlds #19 © 1962 American Comics Group. Art by Ogden Whitney.

authors: #1 (John Wyndham—*Day of the Triffids*), #2 (Alfred Bester), #3 (Harlan Ellison, Larry Niven, Frank Herbert), #4 (A. E. van Vogt, Otis Adelbert Kline), #5 (Larry Niven), #6 (Michael Moorcock), and Annual (Stanley Weinbaum). Artists include Neal Adams (#1), Mike Kaluta (#s 1, 2), and Richard Corben (#4). First issue reprints a 1966 story drawn by Al Williamson, Frank Frazetta, Roy Krenkel, and Angelo Torres. Black-and-white magazine.

Unusual Tales

Charlton Comics
1955 November–1965 March
1–49

Science fiction and supernatural tales. Art by Steve Ditko (#s 6–12, 14, 15, 22, 25–27, 29).

Valley of Gwangi

Dell Publishing
1969 December
01-880-912

Adaptation of 1969 movie which featured adventurers stumbling across a giant prehistoric monster, à la *King Kong*. Art by Jack Sparling.

Vanguard Illustrated

Pacific Comics
1983 November–1984 October
1–11

Science fiction anthology with some continuing series. First appearances of the Stargrazers (#2) and Mr. Monster (#7). Art by George Evans (#7).

Vic Torry and His Flying Saucer

Fawcett Publications
1950
1

Aviator Vic Torry encounters a flying saucer from Mercury which has made a forced landing in the desert. The dying alien pilot turns his spaceship over to Vic and his girlfriend Laura, and then the fun begins. Bob Powell drew this 32-page story which was later reprinted in *Mr. Monster's Super-Duper Special #5* (January 1987).

Voyage to the Bottom of the Sea

Dell/Gold Key
1961; 1964 December–1970 April
1230; 1–16

Adventures on the atomic submarine *Seaview* with Captain Lee Crane. First issue adapted the 1961 movie. Remainder of series based on 1964–68 television show. Issue #s 15, 16 are reprints.

Weird Fantasy

EC Comics
1950 May–1953 November
13(#1)–17(#5), 6–22

The companion title to *Weird Science*, the other most influential science fiction comic book of the early 1950s. Adaptations of stories by Ray Bradbury in #s 13, 17–22. Art by Wally Wood (#s 13–17, 5–14), Joe Orlando (#s 9–22), Al Feldstein (#13–17, 6–8), Al Williamson (#s 14–21), and Harvey Kurtzman (#s 13–17, 6).

Weird Science

EC Comics
1950 May–1953 November
12(#1)–15(#4), 5–22

Along with *Weird Fantasy*, perhaps the

Weird Science #2 © 1952 William M. Gaines. Art by Wally Wood.

Weird Worlds Vol. 2 #3
© 1971 Eerie Publications,
Inc.

best science fiction comic book ever
published. Adaptations of stories by
Ray Bradbury in #s 17–22. Art by Wally
Wood (#s 12, 13, 5–22), Joe Orlando (#s
10–22), Al Williamson (#s 15–22), Al
Feldstein (#s 12–15, 5–8), and Harvey
Kurtzman (#s 12–15, 5–7).

Weird Science
Gladstone Publishing
1990 September–1991 March
1–4

Two EC science fiction comics are reprinted in each 64-page issue. Issue #1
(*Weird Science* #22, *Weird Fantasy* #13),

#2 (*Weird Science* #16, *Weird Fantasy*
#17), #3 (*Weird Science* #9, *Weird Fanta-
sy* #14), #4 (*Weird Science-Fantasy* #27,
Weird Fantasy #11).

Weird Science-Fantasy
EC Comics
1954 March–1955 May
23–29

As sales fell on *Weird Science* and *Weird
Fantasy* in late 1953, publisher William
Gaines consolidated both books into
this one title and raised the price to 15
cents in an effort to break even. With
issue #25, he dropped the price back to
ten cents. Highlights include Harlan
Ellison's first professional work (plot for
"Upheaval!" in #24), a special Flying
Saucer Report issue (#26), adaptations
of Ray Bradbury's stories (#s 23, 25), an
adaptation of Eando Binder's "Adam
Link" series about an intelligent robot
(#s 27, 28), and a cover by Frank
Frazetta (#29) which was originally
intended as a Buck Rogers cover for
Famous Funnies but was rejected as being too violent.

Weird Tales Of The Future
Stanley P. Morse/Aragon Publishing
1952 March–1953 July
1–8

Harry Kantor, whose writing career
spanned radio (*Amos and Andy*), TV
(*George Gobel Show*), and movies (*Artists
and Models, The Rose Tatoo,* etc.), spent
a year of his life as editor and writer of
comic books published by Stanley P.
Morse. Highlights of this title are the
stories written and drawn by Basil Wolverton (#s 2–5). For issue #7, Kantor
reworked Wolverton's "Brain Bats of
Venus" from *Mr. Mystery* #7 and published it as "The Mind Movers."

Weird Thrillers

Ziff-Davis Publications

1951 September–1952 October

1–5

Science fiction and suspense fantasy in stories by Murphy Anderson (#2), Joe Kubert (#4), and Bob Powell (#s 3, 5).

Weird Wonder Tales

Marvel Comics

1973 December–1977 May

1–22

Reprints of 1950s and 1960s suspense and fantasy stories. Highlights include Basil Wolverton's "Eye of Doom" (#1) and art by Bill Everett (#s 3, 6, 9, 16–18), Jack Kirby (#s 6, 11, 13, 16–22), and Steve Ditko (#s 4, 5, 10–13, 19–21).

Weird Worlds

Eerie Publications

1970 December–1971 August

Vol. 1 #10, Vol. 2 #4

A typical story ("The Metal Replacements") is engagingly summarized on the contents page as being about "Man's desire to create metal slaves is realized only to feel the terror of metal slaves wanting to become men. A futurist-weirdo." Volume 2 #3 features "The Evil Trip," about a psychedelics-ingesting scientist. Half horror content with some reprints. Black-and-white magazine.

Weird Worlds

DC Comics

1972 August–1974 October

1–10

Edgar Rice Burroughs's fantasy characters, "John Carter, Warlord of Mars" and "David Innes of Pellucidar," shared the spotlight in issue #s 1–7. Marv Wolfman adapted Burroughs's *Gods of Mars* (with art by Murphy Anderson in #s 1–3), while Denny O'Neil adapted *At the Earth's Core.* Issue #s 8–10 feature Howard Chaykin's swashbuckling space pirate, Iron Wolf.

World of Fantasy

Marvel Comics

1956 May–1959 August

1–19

After the EC science fiction line folded, several artists, such as Berni Krigstein (#9), Joe Orlando (#s 8, 13, 14), and Al Williamson (#s 2, 16), drew stories for this title. Art also by Jack Kirby (#s 16–19), Steve Ditko (#s 16–19), and Sid Check (#3).

World of Wood

Eclipse Comics

1986–89

1–5

Issue #s 1–4 reprint science fiction, fantasy, and adventure stories by Wally Wood from magazines of the 1960s

Weird Wonder Tales #2 © 1974 Marvel Entertainment Group, Inc.

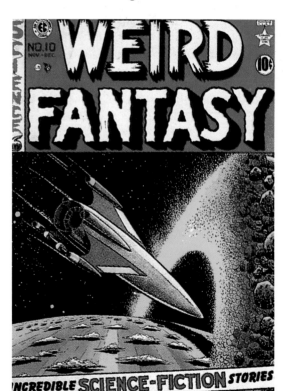

Weird Fantasy #10 © 1952 William M. Gaines. Art by Al Feldstein.

World of Wood © 1986 Cover art Wood/Blevins/Williamson. Art by Wally Wood.

and 1970s. Stories originally published in black and white were colored for this series. Issue #5 reprints (in black and white) a 1950 Wood comic book *Flying Saucers.*

Worlds Unknown
Marvel Comics
1973 May–1974 August
1–8

Adaptations of classic science fiction stories: #1 (Frederik Pohl, Edmond Hamilton), #2 (L. Sprague de Camp, Keith Laumer), #4 (Fredric Brown), #5 (A. E. van Vogt), and #6 (Theodore Sturgeon). Issue #s 7 and 8 are based on the 1974 movie *Golden Voyage of Sinbad.* In issue #3, writer Roy Thomas adapted Harry Bates's 1940 story "Farewell to the Master," which was the basis for the 1951 movie *The Day the Earth Stood Still.* Thomas made the comic book version a more faithful adapta-

tion of the story than did the movie. "After much thought and soul-searching," Thomas noted, "I even left the robot's name as Gnut, as author Bates had originally penned it, in the interest of fidelity—despite the fact that this word can look and sound a bit humorous to those who have a bent that way."

Xenozoic Tales
Kitchen Sink Press
1987 February–1991
1–11+

The Xenozoic Age is five hundred years into the future, when a geological upheaval has changed the Earth into in a "prehistoric" planet where Cadillacs and dinosaurs coexist. Written and drawn by Mark Schultz, the series knits a variety of science fiction comic book themes and styles into a freshly engaging perspective. Black and white.

Xenozoic Tales #2 © 1987 Mark Schultz. Art by Mark Schultz.

BIBLIOGRAPHY

Aldiss, Brian W. *Trillion Year Spree: The History of Science Fiction.* New York: Atheneum, 1986.

Anderson, Murphy. Interview. *Comics Feature* #10, July (1981).

Anderson, Murphy. "Murphy Anderson Talks About Buck Rogers." *Amazing Heroes* #154, December 1 (1988).

Ash, Brian, editor. *The Visual Encyclopedia of Science Fiction.* New York: Harmony Books, 1977.

Asimov, Isaac. *Asimov on Science Fiction.* New York: Doubleday, 1981.

Bails, Jerry and Hames Ware, ed. *Who's Who of American Comic Books.* St. Claire Shores, Michigan: Jerry Bails, 1974.

Benton, Mike. *The Comic Book In America: An Illustrated History.* Dallas, Texas: Taylor Publishing Company, 1989.

——. *Comic Book Collecting For Fun and Profit.* New York: Crown Publishers, 1985.

——. *Horror Comics: The Illustrated History.* Dallas, Texas: Taylor Publishing Company, 1991.

——. *Superhero Comics of the Silver Age.* Dallas, Texas: Taylor Publishing Company, 1991.

Bester, Alfred. Interview. *Comics Interview* #32 (1986).

Boatner, E. R. "Good Lord! Choke . . . Gasp . . . It's EC!" *Comic Book Price Guide* #9 (1979).

Dille, Robert C., editor. *The Collected Works of Buck Rogers in the 25th Century.* New York: A&W Publishers, Inc., 1977.

Ellington, Richard. "Me To Your Leader Take." *All in Color For a Dime.* Eds. Dick Lupoff and Don Thompson. Ace Book, 1970.

Feldstein, Al. Interview. *Squa Tront* #9 (1983).

Fox, Gardner. Interview. *Comics Interview* #9, May (1984).

Fox, Gardner. Interview. *Amazing Heroes* #113, March 15 (1987).

Frewin, Anthony. *One Hundred Years of Science Fiction Illustration.* London: Jupiter Books, 1974.

Gaines, William. Interview. *Comics Journal* #81, May (1983).

Gaines, William et al. "The Science Fiction Panel." *Squa Tront* #8 (1978).

Gerber, Ernst and Mary. *The Photo-Journal Guide to Comic Books.* 2 vols. Minden, Nevada: Gerber Publishing Company, 1989, 1990.

Gifford, Denis. *The International Book of Comics.* New York: Crescent Books, 1984.

Goulart, Ron, editor. *The Encyclopedia of American Comics.* New York: Facts on File, 1990.

Gunn, James. *Alternate Worlds: The Illustrated History of Science Fiction.* Englewood Cliffs, New Jersey: Prentice-Hall, Inc., 1975.

Harrison, Harry. Interview. *Graphic Story Magazine* #15, Summer (1973).

Horn, Maurice, editor. *World Encyclopedia of Comics.* New York: Chelsea House Publishers, 1976.

Jurgens, Dan. Interview. *Amazing Heroes* #137, March 15 (1988).

Krenkel, Roy G. Interview. *Comics Interview* #4, June (1983).

Lillian, Guy H., III. "Strange Schwartz Stories." *Amazing World of DC Comics* #3, November (1974).

Lundwall, Sam. *Science Fiction: An Illustrated History.* New York: Grosset & Dunlap, Inc., 1978.

Nicholls, Peter, editor. *The Science Fiction Encyclopedia.* New York: Doubleday, 1979.

O'Neill, Patrick Daniel. "Panels and Frames." *Comics Scene* #5, September (1982).

O'Neill, Patrick Daniel. "Magnus, Robot Fighter." *Comics Scene* #18, April (1991).

Orlando, Joe. Interview. *Amazing World of DC Comics* #6, May (1975).

Overstreet, Robert M. *Overstreet Comic Book Price Guide*. Cleveland, Tennessee: Overstreet Publications, 1991.

Schwartz, Julius. Interview. *Amazing World of DC Comics* #14, March (1977).

Schwartz, Julius. Interview. *Comics Interview* #88 (1990).

Shapiro, Marc. "Passing the Buck." *Starlog*. December (1990).

Sheridan, Martin. *Classic Comics and Their Creators*. Arcadia, California: Post-Era Books, 1942, 1973.

Spiegle, Dan. Interview. *Graphic Story World*. July (1972).

Stewart, Bhob. "Memories of Wally Wood." *Comics Journal* #70, January (1982).

Stewart, Bhob. "Spawn of the Twin Planets." *Fanfare* #4, Summer (1981).

Uslan, Michael, editor. *Mysteries in Space*. New York: Simon and Schuster, 1980.

Van Hise, James. *The Art of Al Williamson*. San Diego, California: Blue Dolphin Enterprises, 1983.

Van Hise, James. "Magnus, Robot Fighter 4000 A.D." *Comics Feature* #54, April (1987).

Weist, Jerry. "E.C. Science Fiction Comics." *Squa Tront* #3 (1969).

Williamson, Al. "Al Williamson on Flash Gordon." *Amazing Heroes* #137, March 15 (1988).

———. Interview. *Comics Journal* #90, May (1984).

———. "With Alex on Mongo." *Flash Gordon* #1. Princeton, Wisconsin: Kitchen Sink Press, (1990).

Wolfman, Marv and Mike Barr. Interview. *Amazing Heroes* #31, September 15 (1983).

Wolverton, Basil. Interview. *Graphic Story Magazine* #14, Winter (1971).

INDEX